GOOD BITE™
weeknight meals
Delicious Made Easy

GOOD BITE™
weeknight meals
Delicious Made Easy

Photography by Matt Armendariz

Edited by Sepideh Saremi

WILEY

JOHN WILEY & SONS, INC.

For general information about our other products and services, please contact our Custom-
er Care Department within the United States at (800) 762-2974, outside the United States at
(317) 572-3993 or fax (317) 572-4002.

Wiley also publishes its books in a variety of electronic formats. Some content that appears
in print may not be available in electronic books. For more information about Wiley products, visit our web site at www.wiley.com.

Library of Congress Cataloging-in-Publication Data

Good Bite weeknight meals : delicious made easy / photography by Matt Armendariz.
    p. cm.
Includes index.
ISBN 978-0-470-91658-2 (cloth)
1. Dinners and dining. 2. Quick and easy cooking. I. GoodBite.com. II. Title: Weeknight
meals.
 TX737.G57 2011
 641.5'55--dc22

                                        2010037999

Printed in China
10 9 8 7 6 5 4 3 2 1

To food bloggers everywhere. Thanks for leading us back into our kitchens.

CONTENTS

ACKNOWLEDGMENTS

Good Bite is grateful to all the people whose hard work has made this book possible.

Thank you to each of the bloggers who contribute to Good Bite and to those who participated in this book; there never would have been a GoodBite.com without you.

Thank you to our photographer, Matt Armendariz; food stylist, Adam Pearson; prop stylist, Emily Henson; and food stylist assistant, Jenny Park. Your beautiful photos speak for themselves.

Thank you to Sepideh Saremi, our talented editor. Sepi, this book would never have come together without your multitude of talents.

Thank you to Stacey Glick, our tireless agent, and Justin Schwartz, our editor at John Wiley and Sons. And a special thanks to Shauna Ahern, who graciously made those introductions.

Thank you to our terrific team at DECA, who launched the Good Bite website and video series and continue to keep things running smoothly: Michael Wayne, Chris Kimbell, Christian Sanz, Beth Le Manach, Kat Odell, and the whole gang. Special thanks to Katie Hall, who was helpful in selecting the recipes for this book.

And last but certainly not least, thank you to all the users, viewers, and readers of Good Bite, who have made the site what it is today and are the reason this book came to be.

INTRODUCTION

If you are wondering what to cook for dinner tonight—or if you're wondering whether you have the time or energy to cook dinner at all—this book is for you.

Good Bite Weeknight Meals: Delicious Made Easy grew out of GoodBite.com, a website and online series that launched in 2009 to bring the world's best food bloggers together on video. With more than a million visitors each month, Good Bite's original format of a roundtable of bloggers talking about their favorite recipes has expanded to nearly a dozen different video series, all devoted to simple, good cooking.

Since the very beginning, Good Bite's motto and mandate has been "delicious made easy"—to us, that has always meant good, fulfilling food that is prepared simply and quickly, with recipes that are approachable for beginners while still being appealing to more seasoned home cooks. While cooking dinner after a long day might feel like a burden to you, we promise that this book will make it easy and even fun. And it will certainly be delicious.

The Good Bite Philosophy:
DELICIOUS MADE EASY

Spending an hour on a perfectly planned meal can be interesting and satisfying, but on most weeknights it's unrealistic, if not impossible. All of the 141 recipes in *Good Bite Weeknight Meals* were developed by busy people in their own home kitchens. None of the dishes are high-flying or unachievable (though some will seem downright impressive). Recipes were put to the test in real-life situations, complete with long workdays, late meetings, homework, conflicting schedules, and picky eaters.

Each recipe in this book is satisfying, delicious, and simple. Most recipes call for between 5 and 10 ingredients, and very few require more than 15 to 30 minutes of hands-on time. You'll get speedy comfort food like One-Pot, Stove-Top Macaroni and Cheese. Healthy dinners with a contemporary spin, like Halibut Pesto Kabobs. Easy renditions of exotic favorites, like Better Butter Chicken. Many of the recipes focus on fresh ingredients, though some are perfect for those nights when you're low on fresh ingredients and need to dip into your pantry stockpile. While most of these recipes can be prepared right before you're ready to serve them, we've also included a few slow-cooker favorites that require just a tiny bit of planning but are still quite easy to whip together.

HOW THIS BOOK *Is Set Up*

The recipes in this book are divided into eight chapters—Chicken & Turkey, Beef & Lamb, Pork, Seafood, Pasta, Vegetarian, Soups & Stews, and Side Dishes. About half of the recipes include Make It Easy tips—quick tricks from our bloggers that they use in preparing these dishes. Wherever possible, we've provided substitutions for ingredients that might not be readily available, and suggestions for ways to make these dishes your own. We've also included serving suggestions for many of our main dishes, so you don't have to think about what might work with a certain dish.

The Good Bite Pantry:
QUICK MEALS, EVERY NIGHT

For last-minute meals that taste like planned ones, a well-stocked pantry (and fridge and freezer) will be your best friend. In this section, we list most of the items you'll need for the recipes in this book. That includes nonperishable staples as well as items worth seeking out at specialty foods stores and Asian, Indian, and Latin grocers. To help stock the fridge, we've listed versatile and handy ingredients that are smart to have on hand for the recipes in this book as well as for snacking; you can tailor this list depending on your personal taste and how often you shop. We've listed basic produce items that don't need refrigeration and have a relatively long shelf life; these, too, will be useful for both cooking and snacking. And finally, you'll also find key ingredients to keep stashed in the freezer. An ample freezer stash is a lifesaver for the days you just can't make it to the store.

BASIC PRODUCE

Avocados
Apples
Bananas
Cabbage (red or green)
Carrots
Celery
Cherry tomatoes
Garlic
Ginger
Lemons
Limes
Onions
Potatoes
Shallots
Sweet potatoes (yams)
Winter squash (kabocha, butternut, or acorn)

BOTTLES, CANS, CARTONS, & JARS

Artichoke hearts (marinated)
Beans (black, great northern, kidney, navy, pinto, refried)
Broth (beef, chicken, vegetable)
Chickpeas
Chiles (chipotles in adobo, mild green chiles)
Chunk chicken
Coconut milk
Cream of chicken soup
Cream of mushroom soup
Enchilada sauce
Evaporated milk (low-fat)
Greek salad dressing
Lentils
Marinara sauce
Mushroom soup
Olives (kalamata, picholine)
Pineapple chunks
Tomato paste
Tomato sauces (pizza sauce, spaghetti sauce)
Tomatoes (diced, whole, sun-dried; diced tomatoes mixed with mild green chiles)
Tuna
Water chestnuts

CONDIMENTS, SAUCES, & ENHANCERS

Barbecue sauce
Candied ginger
Chili paste (Korean, Thai)
Hoisin sauce
Ketchup
Mayonnaise
Miso paste
Mustard (Dijon, honey, whole grain)
Orange marmalade
Ranch dressing mix (dry)
Soy sauce (low-sodium)
Teriyaki sauce
Sriracha sauce (chili sauce)
Tabasco sauce (or other hot sauce)
Thai chili sauce
Wasabi paste
Worcestershire sauce

FREEZER

Artichoke hearts
Bacon
Beef (flank steak, ground beef, skirt steak)
Broccoli florets
Chicken breast (boneless skinless)
Chicken thighs (boneless skinless)
Corn
Edamame
Fruit juice concentrates (apple, orange, pineapple)
Mixed vegetables
Pearl onions
Peas
Pizza dough
Pork tenderloin
Puff pastry
Sausage (kielbasa, pork, sweet Italian, turkey)
Shrimp (precooked)
Spinach (chopped)
Turkey burgers
Whole grain bread
Wonton wrappers

FRIDGE

Butter
Cheeses (Cheddar, feta, goat's milk, mozzarella, Muenster, Parmesan, Monterey Jack, provolone, Swiss)
Cottage cheese
Deli meats (chicken breast, ham, prosciutto, smoked turkey)
Eggs

"A well-stocked pantry (and fridge and freezer) will be your best friend."

"It's smart to have versatile and handy ingredients in stock."

Milk
Sour cream
Tofu
Tortillas (corn, flour)
Yogurt

GRAINS, PASTA, & STARCHES
Breadcrumbs
Cornstarch
Couscous
Flour (all-purpose)
Lentils
Noodles (chow mein, soba, rice stick)
Oats (old-fashioned rolled)
Pancake mix
Panko (Japanese breadcrumbs)
Pasta (farfalle, lasagna noodles, linguine, macaroni, penne, spaghetti)
Polenta (quick-cooking)
Quinoa (regular or red)
Rice (arborio, jasmine, brown)
Taco shells
Tortilla chips

HERBS & SPICES
Basil
Bay leaf
Cayenne pepper
Chili powder
Cinnamon (ground)
Cajun or Creole seasoning
Chinese five-spice powder

Cumin (ground)
Curry powder
Dill
Garam masala
Garlic salt
Ginger (ground)
Marjoram
Mustard powder
Nutmeg (ground and whole)
Old Bay seasoning
Oregano
Paprika
Red pepper flakes
Salt (kosher or sea)
Seasoned salt
Taco seasoning
Yellow mustard seeds

LIQUOR
Beer
Bourbon
Cognac
Dry sherry
Port
Tequila
Wine (red and white)

NUTS, SEEDS, & DRIED FRUIT
Almonds (sliced and whole)
Cashews (unsalted)
Cherries
Currants
Flax seeds (ground)
Peanuts (roasted)

Pine nuts
Raisins (golden and dark)
Sunflower seeds
Walnuts

OILS
Canola oil
Grapeseed oil
Nonstick cooking spray
Olive oil (extra-virgin, regular)
Toasted sesame oil
Vegetable oil

VINEGARS
Apple cider vinegar
Balsamic vinegar (regular and white)
Red wine vinegar
Rice vinegar
White wine vinegar

SWEETENERS
Honey
Molasses
Sugar (brown and white)

Favorite SECRET INGREDIENTS

We asked the Good Bite bloggers for some of their favorite secret ingredients and to explain their tricks for making the most of them. Now that you've got your pantry set up, here are a few special items to consider (and a few new ways to use more common items that you've probably got in stock now).

Marc Matsumoto, norecipes.com

Kombu dashi powder

I always have packets of kombu dashi (kelp stock) powder on hand. It adds umami, or savoriness, to a dish, and for that I like sprinkling it into soups, stews, and sauces. You can find kombu dashi powder in Japanese grocery stores. Make sure you read the translated label on the back, as there are many different kinds of dashi. (Some of them contain MSG, so it's good to watch out for that, as well.)

Black cardamom

Black cardamom is related to green cardamom, but it has a very different appearance and flavor. The seed pods are much larger than green cardamom and they have an intensely smoky flavor. I love adding it to vegetarian soups and stews, as it adds a meaty flavor that will make you wonder if some bacon fell into the pot. Black cardamom is also a great way to add smokiness to a dish when you don't have a barbecue handy.

Sugar

I know this seems like an obvious ingredient, but it's amazing how a pinch of sugar can drastically change the balance of a dish. In our Japanese household, my mom always added sugar and mirin (sweet Japanese rice wine) to soups and sauces. It always seemed like a normal thing to do until I left the house and started getting funny looks when I added sugar to my chicken stock. I also add a bit of sugar to tomato sauces to balance out the acidity of canned tomatoes and bring out the fruity flavors. When something doesn't taste quite right, but I can't put my finger on the problem, I almost always start by adding a bit of sugar.

Laura Levy, laurasbestrecipes.com

Chipotles

I use a lot of chipotles. The smoke-dried jalapeño peppers are great in all kinds of savory dishes, and sometimes I'll use just the adobo sauce from the can. A spoonful of adobo sauce is so good when you want to add a touch of smoky flavor to sauces or condiments.

Lemongrass

I love using a little bit of lemongrass in soups and seafood dishes. It makes dishes taste so fresh and vibrant and really complements spicy ingredients like Thai chili or jalapeño pepper.

Masa harina

Masa harina, a traditional flour used in Mexican cooking, is very important in my kitchen. I use it in place of regular flour when I want to thicken soups or chilis. It also works well to dredge meat for browning. I also use it to make corn tortillas. I prefer my corn tortillas homemade; they only take a few minutes to make and taste so much better than what you buy at the grocery store.

Sara Wells, ourbestbites.com

Lemons and limes

I always keep fresh lemons and limes on hand in my kitchen. Fresh citrus is the most versatile ingredient I know. It brightens up so many simple dishes, from pasta to grilled meats and fresh vegetables to beverages and desserts. Even a simple, semi-homemade dish is instantly improved with a squeeze of fresh citrus juice added right before serving.

Precooked bacon

I buy precooked sliced bacon in bulk and keep it handy in the fridge. It takes less than a minute to heat up and saves me the mess of pan-frying each time I want to use bacon. That makes it much easier to incorporate bacon in weeknight cooking, whether it's slipped into a sandwich or wrap or sprinkled on salads or pasta, egg, and vegetable dishes.

Kate Jones, **ourbestbites.com**

Garlic

I almost always double the garlic in recipes that call for fresh garlic. I find that the intensity of garlic mellows when it's cooked, so those few extra cloves add so much more flavor.

Bread-machine yeast

I use bread machine yeast in all of my bread baking, even when I'm not using a bread machine. It tends to be less temperamental than other types of yeast and I get more consistent results with less effort.

Marjoram

Marjoram is one of those overlooked spices. Sometimes you'll buy a jar for one specific recipe and then completely forget about it because so few recipes call for it. I love it, though; it rounds out a lot of Italian-style dishes, and many times when I'm making something that calls for Italian seasoning, I'll toss in a little marjoram for good measure. Try sprinkling a little on a pizza right before you slip it into the oven or into a hoagie-style sandwich before serving.

Julie Van Rosendaal, **dinnerwithjulie.com**

Pure maple syrup

I grew up with the real thing and have friends who live on maple farms in Ontario, so there is always a jug of pure maple syrup in my fridge. I adore the flavor, and it's also much easier to pour than honey (it's thinner and runnier, and tends not to solidify the way honey does), so I use it in place of honey in most recipes. I also add maple syrup to balsamic vinaigrettes, drizzle it on roasted sweet potatoes, and use it to make big batches of granola (all you need to do is toss oats, nuts, and seeds with maple syrup and bake until it's golden brown). We also drizzle maple syrup on plain yogurt, bake it into pies, and even use it to sweeten coffee and tea.

Dried red lentils

As the daughter of a gastroenterologist, I can appreciate beans and lentils for their fantastic fiber content. Dried red lentils cook much more quickly than other dried lentils (in about 10 minutes) and get nice and soft. And because they're so mild in flavor, you can add them to all kinds of things; I'm in the habit of tossing a handful into soups (particularly pureed sweet potato and squash soups), and a friend recently taught me to add a spoonful to my oatmeal in the morning. You can't even tell it's there! I simmer up a batch of red lentils, keep it in the fridge, and add spoonfuls to muffins and other baked goods – red lentils look and taste like oatmeal in a cookie or scone!

Sesame oil

I just love the flavor sesame oil adds to fried rice, dressings, noodle dishes, stir fries, and the like. I don't realize how often I use it until it's gone! Just a drizzle adds a nice toasty flavor to curries, Asian dishes, even hummus (I find tahini doesn't have a strong sesame flavor on its own and sometimes needs a little boost).

TECHNIQUE TIPS

These tips for peeling, chopping, slicing, and dicing will make quick and easy work of otherwise tedious ingredient prep.

Avocados

To dice or slice an avocado, first use a knife to cut the avocado in half lengthwise, and pull the halves apart. Cut the half with the core lengthwise in half again and pull the quarters apart. Remove the pit using a spoon. Then either slice the avocado in its peel or make a cross-hatch pattern if dicing, cutting to (but not through) the skin, and use a spoon to scoop out the pieces or slices. To keep cut avocados from going brown, cover them with plastic wrap, pressing to ensure the plastic wrap makes an air-tight seal with the cut sides.

Beets

The best way to peel beets depends on whether you peel them before or after roasting them. If peeling before roasting, wear kitchen gloves and use a vegetable peeler. If peeling after roasting, which is our preferred method, wait until the beets have cooled and slip off the peel using a couple of paper towels and your fingers.

Bell peppers

Chop off the top of the pepper, chop off the bottom of the pepper, make a lengthwise slice down one side of the pepper, open it up, and pull out the core and seeds. Cut the big piece of pepper into quarters and slice or chop them.

Green beans

Lots of people trim the tapered ends of green beans, but they're perfectly edible and quite pretty, so we like to leave them on. To trim green beans, line them up and use a knife to slice off the tough ends only.

Herbs

A clean pair of kitchen shears will do a fine job of quickly snipping cilantro, chives, and other fresh herbs.

Kale

To remove the thick ribs from kale, place a kale leaf on your cutting board, fold it so the rib is on one side and the leafy parts are touching, and use your knife to carefully carve away the rib, cutting through both leafy parts at once.

Lemons and limes

You'll get the most juice from lemons and limes if they're room temperature. Use the palm of your hand to roll them on the kitchen counter a bit before cutting them open and squeezing them.

Mangoes

To dice a mango, stand it up on its stem end on a cutting board and hold onto it. Cut down one broad side, slightly off-center to avoid the seed, and then do the same on the other side. Then make a cross-hatch pattern in each of the two large pieces you've just sliced, cutting the flesh to (but not through) the skin. Push the pieces inside out and use a small knife or a spoon to remove the mango pieces from the skin.

Onions

The easiest way to chop onions is to use your food processor. Cut off the top and bottom of the onion, remove the skin, and chop it into quarters. Place the quarters in your food processor and pulse a few times until the onion is chopped.

Tomatoes

To dice tomatoes, cut them in half crosswise and squeeze out the juice and seeds. Cut each half in two. Place the pieces on a cutting board, skin side down, and dice.

Weeknight PLANNING & PREP

Though most of the recipes in this book don't require planning, there's an art and a science to successful weeknight cooking. Here are some of the strategies we've learned that help get dinner on the table quickly and painlessly on weeknights.

Plan just a little bit.
We've found that a little bit of planning can go a really long way when it comes to weeknight cooking. Think about the foods you like to cook and plan loose, flexible menus around them. Consider what's going on in your week and plan to make super-fast dishes or make use of your slow-cooker for the nights you know will leave you time-crunched.

Chop, slice, peel, and dice ahead of time.
It often makes sense to do at least some ingredient prep ahead of time, right after you come home from the market. So think about washing, chopping, and peeling whatever you can over the weekend and you'll find yourself much more inclined to cook during the week.

Cook big when you can.
If you know you're going to use an ingredient twice in one week, like brown rice or ground beef, cook twice as much the first time you use it and save the rest for the second time. Some Good Bite bloggers like to make big batches of their favorite ingredients in one go, then refrigerate or freeze for later use.

Rethink your kitchen setup.
Sometimes very simple changes in your kitchen can make all the difference in how often you cook. This doesn't mean you need to remodel. Rather, think carefully about small adjustments that might make prep and cooking faster and easier for you. This could be moving the kitchen trash can closer to the counter so you can clean up as you work, or making sure the herbs and spices are labeled, organized, and within reach (while still being a safe distance from the stove—heat is no good for spices). Other ideas include hanging frequently used pots and pans on the wall or re-arranging kitchen tools so you've always got what you use most often right at hand.

Make friends with your freezer.
We touch on this throughout this book, but we can't stress enough how helpful the freezer can be in weeknight cooking. More items can be frozen than you might think, including many chopped seasonal herbs and veggies. Keep in mind that it makes sense to freeze things in smaller, usable portions—that way you avoid waiting hours for a massive bag of something to defrost when you really just need a little bit for your recipe.

The Good Bite Basics:
10 TIME-SAVING TOOLS

These 10 basic tools deserve special consideration because they make kitchen prep go even faster. Plus, several of the items have multiple uses.

Baking Sheet (Rimmed)

A heavy-duty 18x13-inch rimmed baking sheet is perfect for baking cookies, of course. But it's also great for quick oven roasting and reheating because the sides are shallower than a baking dish, and thus allow for better heat circulation. Inverted and set over two stove burners, a baking sheet also converts to make-shift counter space in a tight kitchen.

Blender

Blenders come in two styles. A stand blender is what you want for making smoothies and blended drinks, and pureed soups. An immersion blender, also known as a stick blender, is smaller, less expensive, and less powerful than a stand blender. If you like to make soups, it's a special boon, as a stick blender allows you to puree the soup in the pot it was cooked in, rather than transferring the soup to a blender jar.

Food Processor

A food processor is made for quick chopping, pulverizing, and grinding. It also comes with attachment disks that grate or slice ingredients like cheese, carrots, and potatoes in a fraction of the time that it takes to grate by hand. A mini food processor, with a work bowl that's smaller than that of a regular food processor, is ideal for chopping small quantities of herbs or grinding breadcrumbs in seconds.

Garlic Press

A garlic press is a clamplike tool that minces a garlic clove in a single movement, much more quickly than you could mince it with a knife.

Kitchen Shears

A pair of kitchen shears allows you to chop tiny amounts of herbs like parsley, dill, and chives quickly by simply snipping them right from the stem, instead of chopping with a knife and cutting board.

Kitchen shears are also good for cutting pizza and, of course, great for opening prepackaged food neatly.

Knives

Sharp, top-tier knives last forever. What's more, they make slicing and chopping safer and quicker because they'll do it with less effort. You don't need a big array. Start with a 6-inch chef's knife, a 3-inch paring knife, and a serrated knife (great for bread, citrus, and tomatoes). It's worth the time to visit a cookware store and try out a few different knives to see which feels most comfortable in your hand.

Microplane Grater

With sharp, fine teeth similar to a carpenter's rasp, this handy tool grates citrus zest in seconds. It also makes quick work of grating ginger, garlic, and small amounts of Parmesan cheese.

Nonstick Skillet

Nonstick skillets clean up more quickly than conventional ones. They're superb for cooking frittatas, scrambled eggs, and fish, and for any kind of skillet cooking where you want to use less fat. In response to concerns about toxic chemicals released by certain nonstick coatings at high heat, cookware companies have come up with new "green" pans, whose non-Teflon linings appear to be safer than those of earlier generations of nonstick pans.

Parchment Paper

Lining a rimmed baking sheet with parchment paper keeps food from sticking to the pan and makes cleanup easier. Bakers use parchment paper, but it's also good for roasting vegetables in a low or medium oven (below 400°F).

Spring-Loaded Tongs

Many cooks consider a pair of sturdy tongs an extension of their hands. No tool is better for moving pork chops or chicken breasts around a skillet and transferring them to plates; tongs are great for tossing salad and pasta, too.

ONE
Chicken & Turkey

Teriyaki Chicken *by Todd Porter and Diane Cu,* whiteonricecouple.com

1 cup crushed pineapple chunks (from 20-ounce can)

½ cup pineapple juice (from 20-ounce can)

½ cup low-sodium soy sauce

1 1-inch knob fresh ginger, peeled and minced

1 garlic clove, minced

2 tablespoons brown sugar

½ teaspoon apple cider vinegar

½ teaspoon toasted sesame oil

1 tablespoon cornstarch

1 tablespoon cold water

½ cup vegetable oil

2 pounds boneless skinless chicken breasts

Of course, you can always buy teriyaki sauce. But if you've never made your own, this recipe will convert you forever. Quick, simple, and free of excess salt or preservatives, this teriyaki sauce can also be modified slightly to use as a marinade, as we've done here. *Serves 4 to 6*

Place the pineapple chunks, pineapple juice, soy sauce, ginger, garlic, brown sugar, vinegar, and sesame oil in a blender and blend on high for a few seconds until the teriyaki mixture is well combined. In a small bowl, mix the cornstarch and cold water, breaking clumps with a fork until smooth; set aside. Transfer the teriyaki mixture to a large saucepan over medium heat and bring to a boil, about 10 minutes. Remove from the heat and add the cornstarch mixture, stirring rapidly until the sauce thickens, 1 to 2 minutes. Let the sauce cool, about 5 minutes. (This yields about 1 cup of sauce; reserve ½ cup to serve.)

To make the marinade, place ½ cup teriyaki sauce and the vegetable oil in a large bowl, whisking until combined. Add the chicken breasts and marinate for 20 minutes.

Prepare the grill or grill pan to medium-high. Remove the chicken from the marinade and discard the marinade. Grill the chicken, turning occasionally, until just cooked through, about 10 minutes. Remove the chicken from the grill and serve with the reserved teriyaki sauce.

MAKE IT EASY

It's easy to adjust the teriyaki sauce to suit your taste—if it's too thick for you, just dilute it with water; and try experimenting with the amount of ginger and garlic you add. You can make the sauce ahead of time; it will keep in the fridge, covered, for up to 2 weeks.

Pan-Seared Chicken Breasts with Roasted Mushrooms, Olives, & Red Peppers

by Shauna James Ahern and Daniel Ahern, glutenfreegirl.com

This recipe works best when you cook bone-in chicken breasts with part of the wing still remaining, known in the culinary world as an "airline breast." You can find these at a good butcher's shop or you can ask the butcher at your grocery store to cut the breasts this way for you. Roasting the breast with the wing still attached means a juicier piece of chicken. Nobody likes a dried-out chicken breast. We prefer using Spanish sherry in this recipe. *Serves 4*

Preheat the oven to 450°F. Heat 2 tablespoons of the canola oil in a large sauté pan over medium-high heat. Add 2 of the chicken breasts, skin side down, and cook until golden-brown, about 4 minutes per side. Transfer the seared chicken breasts to a large baking dish and let them rest. Repeat with the remaining canola oil and chicken breasts.

Transfer the seared chicken breasts to the oven and bake until the juices run clear and the internal temperature of the chicken, taken where the wing bone is connected to the breast, is 155°F, about 15 minutes.

While the chicken breasts bake, add the olive oil to the hot sauté pan. Add the mushrooms and bell peppers to the pan and cook over medium-high heat, stirring, until the mushrooms are golden-brown and have released their moisture, about 5 minutes. Add the garlic, thyme, and olives, and cook until fragrant, about 2 minutes.

Add the sherry to deglaze the pan, scraping browned bits from the bottom. Cook until the sherry is reduced by one-third, about 3 minutes. Add the butter and cook, swirling the pan, until the sauce has emulsified, about 1 minute. Taste the sauce and season to taste with salt and pepper. To serve, place a cooked chicken breast on each plate and top with the mushroom mixture.

4 tablespoons canola oil, divided
4 chicken breasts with skin and bones (see Headnote)
3 tablespoons olive oil
2 cups quartered button mushrooms
2 red bell peppers, stemmed, seeded, and chopped
1 heaping tablespoon chopped garlic
2 tablespoons finely chopped fresh thyme
¾ cup pitted kalamata olives
1 cup dry sherry
2 tablespoons unsalted butter
Salt and freshly ground black pepper

"What I learned from my mother about weeknight cooking is to have some basic family favorites in your back pocket—nutritious meals that are easy to make and don't require too much prep—and then improvise!"

–Elise Bauer

Elise Bauer, simplyrecipes.com

Elise Bauer is the blogger and photographer behind the food blog Simply Recipes (simplyrecipes.com), where she has been documenting her journey of learning to cook with her parents since 2003. She has been featured in *Time* magazine, the *Boston Globe*, *Redbook*, and the *London Times* online. Elise lives in Carmichael, California, where she grows her own tomatoes, zucchini, cucumbers, pomegranates, kiwifruit, lemons, walnuts, apples, figs, plums, grapes, and nectarines. She does not raise her own chickens. Yet.

More About Elise

What do you always have in your shopping cart?
Corn tortillas. Seriously! And avocados. Don't ever want to be without them.

What's your go-to weeknight dinner?
Tuna macaroni salad. I grew up eating it every Friday (we're Catholic, so we had fish on Fridays) and it's still one of my favorite comfort foods. It takes as much time as boiling macaroni.

What's your favorite kitchen tool?
Now that I have a cherry pitter, you'll have to pry it from my cold, dead hands.

Is there anything you just can't eat?
Menudo. And not for lack of trying. It's just not my thing.

Roasted Chicken Thighs with Mango Chutney Sauce *by Elise Bauer,* simplyrecipes.com

- 2 pounds chicken thighs with skin and bones, trimmed of excess fat
- Salt and freshly ground black pepper
- 1 tablespoon olive oil
- 1 medium onion, chopped
- 1 tablespoon chopped fresh or candied ginger
- 2 ripe but firm mangoes, peeled and cubed into ½-inch pieces
- ½ cup water
- ¼ cup distilled white vinegar
- ¼ cup sugar
- 1 garlic clove, minced
- 2 teaspoons chopped raisins
- ½ teaspoon yellow mustard seeds
- ¼ teaspoon red pepper flakes
- Hot cooked rice (optional)
- Cooked peas (optional)

This bright and flavorful dish is simple to make, but looks and tastes as though you spent all day in the kitchen. The sweet tang of the chutney complements the dark and juicy thigh meat; try serving it alongside hot cooked rice and bright green peas to make the flavors and colors pop even more. This dish also keeps well, so you can make it ahead and reheat for guests. *Serves 4*

Preheat the oven to 400°F. Season the chicken with salt and pepper. Heat the oil in a large skillet over medium-high heat until the oil shimmers and begins to smoke slightly. Place the chicken in the skillet, skin side down. Sear until golden-brown, 4 to 5 minutes per side. Remove the chicken from the skillet and place in a roasting pan. Roast in the oven on the center rack until the chicken is cooked, 30 minutes.

While the chicken is roasting, drain all but 1 tablespoon of fat from the pan. Add the onion and cook over medium-high heat until the onion is softened, about 5 minutes. Add the ginger and cook for 1 minute, then add the mangoes, water, vinegar, sugar, garlic, raisins, mustard seeds, and red pepper flakes and stir. Bring the sauce to a simmer and reduce the heat to low. Cover, cook for 10 minutes, and remove the chutney from the heat. Remove the chicken from the oven and serve with the mango chutney sauce and hot cooked rice and peas, if desired.

Garlic Chicken Stir-Fry *by Lori Lange,* recipegirl.com

I've been making this chicken stir-fry for as long as I can remember. It was a staple in my mother's cooking rotation, and it's become a regular in my own home now, too. A ginger-soy sauce is stir-fried with fresh vegetables, chicken, cashews, and plenty of garlic. Served over rice, it's a healthier version of the cashew chicken that you might find in an Asian restaurant. *Serves 4*

Place the chicken broth, soy sauce, cornstarch, and ginger in a small bowl and stir until combined. Set aside.

Heat 2 tablespoons of the oil in a large skillet over medium-high heat. Add the chicken and garlic and stir-fry until the chicken turns white, about 3 minutes. Add the remaining 1 tablespoon oil, the bell pepper, snow peas, cashews, and scallions and stir-fry for 1 minute.

Reduce the heat to medium, add the chicken-broth mixture, and bring to a boil, stirring. Boil until the mixture thickens, about 1 minute. Serve immediately with the hot cooked rice.

½ cup chicken broth

2 tablespoons low-sodium soy sauce

1 tablespoon cornstarch

½ teaspoon ground ginger

3 tablespoons canola oil, divided

1 pound boneless skinless chicken breasts, cut into 1-inch pieces

4 garlic cloves, minced

1 large red bell pepper, stemmed, seeded, and chopped

½ cup snow peas

¼ cup unsalted cashews

¼ cup sliced scallions

Hot cooked rice

Better Butter Chicken *by Julie Van Rosendaal,* dinnerwithjulie.com

This recipe is a great way to use up leftover roast chicken or turkey; chop it up and add it to the sauce instead of cooking fresh chicken breasts or thighs. Don't use fat-free yogurt in this recipe, as it tends to separate when cooked, particularly with tomato sauce. *Serves 4*

Heat 1 tablespoon of the oil in a large skillet over medium-high heat. Add the chicken and cook until golden-brown, 2 to 3 minutes per side. Remove the chicken from the pan and set aside.

Add the remaining 1 tablespoon oil to the skillet, add the onion, and cook until it begins to brown, about 5 minutes. Add the ginger and garlic and cook for 1 minute, then add the chili powder and cinnamon and cook for 1 more minute. Slice the chicken on a slight diagonal. Add the tomatoes and tomato paste to the pan and bring to a simmer. Add the chicken slices to the skillet, cover, and simmer until the sauce has thickened and the chicken is fully cooked, 20 to 30 minutes. Reduce the heat to low and add the garam masala, yogurt, and cream and stir. Season to taste with salt and pepper and serve immediately over the hot cooked rice.

- 2 tablespoons canola or olive oil, divided
- 1½ pounds boneless skinless chicken breasts or boneless skinless chicken thighs
- 1 medium onion, finely chopped
- 1 tablespoon grated fresh ginger
- 3 garlic cloves, crushed
- 2 teaspoons chili powder
- ¼ teaspoon ground cinnamon
- 1 19-ounce can diced tomatoes, undrained
- 2 tablespoons tomato paste
- 2 teaspoons garam masala (optional)
- 1 cup plain yogurt
- ½ cup half-and-half or heavy whipping cream, or to taste
  Salt and freshly ground black pepper
  Hot cooked basmati rice

MAKE IT EASY
Freeze any leftover tomato paste in spoonfuls on waxed paper, then transfer to a freezer bag to add directly to soups, sauces, and stews.

Grilled Chicken Tacos *by Rachel Rappaport,* coconutandlime.com

Oil, for brushing grill

4 boneless skinless chicken breasts

2 teaspoons ground chipotle chile powder, or to taste

Salt and freshly ground black pepper

2 Cubanelle peppers or fresh Anaheim chiles, seeded and cubed

12 grape or cherry tomatoes

8 6-inch flour tortillas

Grilling peppers and tomatoes alongside your chicken means you can make this entire meal on the grill, and there's no need to run back and forth from the kitchen to the yard to prep salsa or taco toppings while the chicken is cooking. Soak the bamboo skewers in water for 30 minutes before using them, to prevent the skewers from burning. *Serves 4*

Brush the grill rack with oil and prepare the grill to medium.

Season both sides of the chicken breasts with the chipotle chile powder and add salt and freshly ground black pepper. Alternately thread the peppers and tomatoes on bamboo skewers (see Headnote). Place the vegetable skewers and chicken on the grill. Cook until the chicken is fully cooked, turning once, about 10 minutes. Slice the chicken breasts and serve with the grilled vegetables and tortillas.

MAKE IT EASY
Season the chicken the day before grilling or several hours before grilling, and refrigerate until ready to grill.

Rachel Rappaport, coconutandlime.com

Rachel Rappaport started the award-winning food blog Coconut & Lime (coconutandlime.com) in 2004 to share her original recipes with her friends. It quickly became a hit with its focus on unique recipes that incorporate seasonal ingredients, exciting spices, and flavor combinations in a format that even inexperienced home cooks could follow. MSN's Delish.com named Coconut & Lime one of the top 50 food blogs in the world.

Following the success of her blog, Rachel has become a popular food writer, recipe developer, and commentator, appearing in a wide range of online and print publications and on webcasts, television, and radio. Her first cookbook, *The Everything Healthy Slow Cooker Cookbook*, was published in 2010.

More About Rachel

What do you always have in your shopping cart?
I always have tons of fresh, seasonal produce.

What's your go-to weeknight dinner?
I love to make quesadillas with leftover meats or vegetables from earlier dinners. They are perfect for when I need a day off from a creating a new recipe. Risotto is good for the same reason.

What's your favorite kitchen tool?
I love my stand mixer. It makes baking so easy. I can measure out ingredients or clean up while it does the mixing for me.

Is there anything you just can't eat?
I have three foods on my do-not-eat list: ketchup, cantaloupe, and pumpkin pie. Just the smell of those foods makes me feel queasy.

Balsamic Chicken *by Catherine McCord,* **weelicious.com**

¼ cup balsamic vinegar

2 tablespoons olive oil

2 tablespoons Dijon mustard

1 garlic clove, minced

4 boneless skinless chicken
  breasts

Chicken is one of my family's favorite foods because it's not too expensive and it's very easy to prepare with little mess. We're so busy around here that I like to cook a whole bunch of boneless skinless breasts at a time, so we always have a good protein to munch on for lunch or dinner or even as a snack.

I love this versatile recipe because you can triple it to feed a crowd for a summer barbecue or simply make some for dinner and have plenty left over for lunch or an afternoon snack. This recipe is a no-brainer, especially for those who don't like to cook! I like to serve this with a side salad or sautéed broccoli rabe with sliced garlic. *Serves 4*

Place the balsamic vinegar, oil, mustard, and garlic in a large bowl and whisk to combine. Add the chicken breasts, cover, and marinate in the refrigerator for 1 hour or overnight.

Prepare the grill to medium-high. Cook the chicken breasts until golden-brown and fully cooked but still moist, 4 to 5 minutes per side. Serve immediately.

MAKE IT EASY

Make a double batch of the marinade and reserve half of the unused marinade to serve on salad as a dressing. If you don't have a grill, you can bake the chicken breasts in a 375°F oven until they are no longer pink in the center, about 18 minutes, or broil them until they are fully cooked, 6 to 7 minutes per side.

Chicken Salad with Major Grey Chutney

by Andrea Meyers, **andreasrecipes.com**

Major Grey chutney is an Indian condiment—a mango preserve with ginger—that adds a spicy-sweet kick to this chicken salad. You can find Major Grey chutney in well-stocked supermarkets, Indian or international markets, or online.

To make this salad even faster, use leftover roasted chicken. Because of the high heat of the broiler, you'll want to avoid using extra-virgin olive oil in this recipe. *Serves 4*

Place the oven rack about 4 inches below the broiler and preheat to high. Line a 9x13-inch baking dish with foil. Rub the chicken breasts with the oil, place them in the prepared baking dish, and season to taste with sea salt and freshly ground black pepper.

Broil the chicken until the edges are golden, 10 to 12 minutes. Remove the chicken from the oven and let it cool for about 5 minutes, then shred the meat. Place the shredded chicken in a medium bowl and let it cool for 5 more minutes.

While the chicken cools, place the yogurt, chutney, and diced apple in another medium bowl and stir to combine. Add the shredded chicken and toss to combine.

To serve, arrange the lettuce in 4 serving bowls and top with the snow peas and grated carrot. Place scoops of the chicken salad on top of the salad greens. Top with a few currants or raisins and serve.

- 4 boneless skinless chicken breasts, pounded to a ½-inch thickness between two sheets of plastic wrap
- 2 tablespoons olive oil (not extra-virgin)
- ¼ teaspoon sea salt
  Freshly ground black pepper
- ⅔ cup low-fat plain yogurt
- ⅓ cup Major Grey chutney
- 1 small apple, peeled and diced
- 1 small head red leaf lettuce, shredded
- ½ cup snow peas, trimmed and halved
- 1 carrot, peeled and grated
- ¼ cup dried currants or raisins

"I always have simple, quick-to-prepare meals in mind, so I don't add any stress to my already busy week. Keeping the fridge and pantry stocked helps, too!"

—*Jenny Flake*

Inside-Out Chicken Pot Pie *by Jenny Flake,* **picky-palate.com**

1 **sheet frozen puff pastry, thawed**

1 **10.75-ounce can cream of chicken soup**

1 **cup milk**

2 **cups shredded rotisserie chicken**

1½ **cups frozen mixed vegetables (peas, carrots, and corn)**

⅛ **teaspoon salt**

⅛ **teaspoon freshly ground black pepper**

⅛ **teaspoon garlic salt**

4 **sprigs fresh rosemary, for garnish (optional)**

Shred your rotisserie chicken ahead of time and save the extras for another dinner. Try adding ¼ teaspoon Cajun seasoning to the soup mixture for another layer of great flavor. Serves 4

Preheat the oven to 400°F. Carefully unfold the puff pastry onto a clean, lightly floured work surface. Cut the puff pastry into 4 squares and place the squares on an ungreased baking sheet. Pierce the center of each square several times with a fork. Bake until golden-brown, about 15 minutes. Remove from the oven and set aside.

While the puff pastry bakes, place the soup and milk in a large bowl and stir to combine. Transfer the soup mixture to a large skillet over medium heat. Add the chicken, vegetables, salt, pepper, and garlic salt and cook, stirring to break up the chicken pieces, until hot, about 5 minutes.

To serve, place the baked puff pastry squares on plates and top with the hot chicken mixture. Garnish each with a rosemary sprig, if desired.

Cheesy Chicken Cordon Bleu & Rice Casserole *by Jenny Flake,* picky-palate.com

This is a great make-ahead dinner. Prep it the night before, cover it with foil, and refrigerate, then bake the next evening for dinner. Use any cooked rice you like. *Serves 6 to 8*

Preheat the oven to 350°F. Heat the oil in a large skillet over medium heat. Add the onion and bell pepper and cook, stirring, until softened, about 5 minutes. Add the ham, chicken, and garlic and cook, stirring, until warm, about 5 more minutes. Add the melted butter, flour, salt, and pepper, stirring until combined. Add the chicken broth and cooked rice and stir to combine.

Transfer the chicken and rice mixture to a 9x13-inch baking dish. Top with the cheeses and bake until the cheese is melted, 10 to 15 minutes. Remove from the oven, cover with foil, and cook until the cheese is bubbling, about 10 more minutes. Serve immediately.

2 tablespoons extra-virgin olive oil

1 medium onion, finely chopped

1 red bell pepper, stemmed, seeded, and diced

½ pound ham, diced

2 cups shredded cooked boneless skinless chicken breast

1 garlic clove, minced

4 tablespoons (½ stick) butter, melted

¼ cup all-purpose flour

½ teaspoon salt

¼ teaspoon freshly ground black pepper

1 14-ounce can chicken broth

3 cups cooked rice

1 cup shredded Cheddar cheese

1 cup shredded mozzarella or Swiss cheese

Chicken Lettuce Wraps *by Christy Jordan,* southernplate.com

1 cup plus 1 tablespoon vegetable oil, divided

2 ounces rice stick noodles

3 boneless skinless chicken breasts, cut into ½-inch pieces

3 scallions, chopped

1 8-ounce can water chestnuts, drained and finely chopped

1 cup finely chopped button mushrooms

3 tablespoons soy sauce

2 tablespoons brown sugar

8 iceberg or Boston lettuce leaves

I developed this recipe to help combat my personal addiction to some rather expensive chicken lettuce wraps at a local restaurant. In addition to being every bit as delicious, these are a good bit easier to make than I thought and they save us a great deal of money! My husband says he likes them better than the originals they were modeled after. *Serves 4*

Line a plate with paper towels. Heat 1 cup of the oil in a small saucepan over medium heat until very hot. Working in batches, break the rice stick noodles in half and drop them into the pot, cooking until golden and puffy, a couple of seconds. Using a slotted spoon, transfer the noodles to the paper towel–lined plate.

Heat the remaining 1 tablespoon oil in a large skillet over medium heat. Add the chicken and cook, stirring, for 2 minutes. Add the scallions, water chestnuts, and mushrooms and cook, stirring, until the chicken is cooked through and no longer pink in the center, about 5 minutes. Remove from the heat. Finely dice the cooked chicken mixture and return it to the skillet.

Place the soy sauce and brown sugar in a small bowl and stir to combine. Add the sauce to the skillet with the chicken and vegetables and cook, stirring, over medium heat until hot, 2 to 3 minutes. Serve the chicken mixture in the lettuce leaves, topped with the crunchy rice noodles.

©2010 Jennifer Davick

MAKE IT EASY
Substitute about 3 cups leftover cooked chicken or turkey for the chicken breasts. You can also make the rice sticks a day ahead.

Sautéed Chicken with Dill & Tomato Orzo

by Lori Lange, recipegirl.com

1½ **cups orzo**

1 **tablespoon olive oil**

1 **pound marinated boneless skinless chicken breasts (about 2 large), pounded to a ¼-inch thickness between two sheets of plastic wrap**

1 **tablespoon butter**

1½ **cups halved yellow pear tomatoes or cherry tomatoes**

2 **tablespoons chopped fresh dill Salt and freshly ground black pepper**

½ **cup crumbled feta cheese**

1 **small lemon, cut into wedges**

This Greek-style dinner is light and fresh and uses just a handful of ingredients. Tender orzo with tomatoes and fresh dill are combined with feta cheese to provide a base for sautéed chicken. Don't forget to squeeze a lemon wedge on top to bring all of the flavors together. *Serves 4*

Prepare the orzo in a medium saucepan according to the package instructions.

While the orzo cooks, heat the oil in a large skillet over medium-high heat. Add the chicken breasts, cover, and cook until the chicken is golden-brown and no longer pink in the center, about 5 minutes per side.

Drain the cooked orzo and return it to the saucepan. Add the butter, tomatoes, and dill, stirring to combine. Remove the orzo from the heat.

To serve, place the dill and tomato orzo in bowls. Season to taste with salt and pepper. Slice the cooked chicken breasts and place them on top of the orzo; top the chicken with the cheese. Serve with the lemon wedges.

MAKE IT EASY

You should be able to find seasoned/marinated chicken breasts in your supermarket's poultry section. If you just have regular chicken, toss it with some fresh lemon juice, olive oil, dill, salt, and pepper and quick-marinate it for 15 minutes at room temperature (or cover and refrigerate overnight).

Chicken Strips with Honey Mustard

by Julie Van Rosendaal, **dinnerwithjulie.com**

Homemade chicken strips are far better than any packaged frozen variety and almost as easy to prepare. If you prefer, these can be cooked in a hot skillet with a little oil instead of baking them in the oven. Serve them with bottled plum sauce, or stir together equal amounts of honey and mustard for dipping, as we've done here. There are tons of variations for this recipe—have fun with it! *Serves 4*

1 large egg or ½ cup buttermilk
3 boneless skinless chicken breast halves, cut into 1-inch-wide strips
1 to 2 cups panko (Japanese breadcrumbs)
¼ cup freshly grated Parmesan cheese
  Salt and freshly ground black pepper
  Nonstick cooking spray
  Honey
  Yellow or Dijon mustard

Preheat the oven to 375°F. Beat the egg lightly in a large shallow dish. (If you are using buttermilk instead, pour it over the chicken strips in a large bowl and refrigerate for 1 hour.) Place the panko and cheese in another large shallow dish, season to taste with salt and pepper, and stir to combine.

Dredge the chicken strips in the egg (or remove from the buttermilk) and roll in the crumbs to coat well. Lightly spray the prepared chicken strips with non-stick cooking spray and place them on a baking sheet, about 1 inch apart. Bake until the chicken strips are golden and fully cooked, 15 to 20 minutes. In a small bowl, mix equal amounts of honey and mustard to create a dipping sauce. Serve immediately.

MAKE IT EASY

If you don't have panko, use corn flake crumbs, dry breadcrumbs, or finely crushed crackers. Here are other easy variations of this recipe:

Curried-Almond Chicken Fingers: Coat the chicken strips in a mixture of 1½ cups crumbs of your choice (see Make It Easy), ½ cup finely chopped almonds, and 1 teaspoon curry powder.
Pecan-Crusted Chicken Fingers: Coat the chicken strips in a mixture of ¾ cup finely chopped pecans, ½ cup corn flake crumbs or panko (Japanese breadcrumbs), 2 tablespoons flour, and salt and pepper.
Spicy Chicken Fingers: Add 1 teaspoon chili powder to the crumb mixture, and a few drops of Tabasco sauce to the buttermilk.
Crunchy Buffalo Chicken Fingers: Dip the chicken strips in low-fat creamy ranch dressing spiked with 1 teaspoon hot sauce, then roll in crumbs to coat.
Crispy Sesame Chicken Fingers: Roll the chicken strips in a mixture of half crumbs of your choice (see Make It Easy) and half sesame seeds. Serve with sweet-and-sour or sweet garlic dipping sauce.

Braised Moroccan Chicken *by Catherine McCord,* **weelicious.com**

1 tablespoon olive oil

1 small onion, thinly sliced

1 teaspoon paprika

½ teaspoon ground cinnamon

½ teaspoon ground cumin

¼ teaspoon ground ginger

1 teaspoon salt

1 15-ounce can chopped tomatoes, undrained

1 14-ounce can chickpeas, rinsed and drained

1 pound boneless skinless chicken thighs

My son, Kenya, loves helping me measure out the spices for this dish, which takes no time to prepare. The chicken thighs are inexpensive, though you can also use breasts if you have those on hand. Try serving it with a scoop of couscous. *Serves 4*

Heat the oil in a large sauté pan over medium heat. Add the onion and cook, stirring, until translucent, about 5 minutes. Stir in the paprika, cinnamon, cumin, ginger, and salt, then add the tomatoes and bring to a boil. Add the chickpeas and chicken and stir to coat. Reduce the heat to low, cover, and simmer, stirring occasionally, until the chicken is fully cooked, about 20 minutes. Serve immediately.

MAKE IT EASY

Make an extra batch of the spice mixture to have ready for the next time you make this dish. For a lower-fat option, you can use chicken breasts instead of thighs.

Caramelized Onion & Sweet Pepper Turkey Burgers

by Jenny Flake, **picky-palate.com**

Check your supermarket for ground turkey that is preformed into patties, lightly season the patties at home, and they're ready for the grill. I like to serve these with a fresh salad, baked potatoes, or fresh fruit. Try adding a little bit of chopped fresh basil to the mayonnaise to add more flavor. *Serves 4*

Prepare the grill to medium-high. Season the turkey patties with kosher salt and pepper.

Heat the oil in a large skillet over medium heat. Add the onion and bell pepper and cook, stirring, until golden and softened, 7 to 10 minutes. Reduce the heat to low.

Grill the turkey burgers until fully cooked, about 3 minutes per side. Lightly spread the mayonnaise and mustard on the buns and place the cooked burgers on the bun bottoms. Top with the spinach, caramelized onions and peppers, and bun tops. Serve immediately.

- 4 **ground turkey patties, each ½ inch thick**
- **Kosher salt and freshly ground black pepper**
- 2 **tablespoons extra-virgin olive oil**
- 1 **large onion, thinly sliced**
- 1 **large green bell pepper, stemmed, seeded, and chopped**
- **Light mayonnaise**
- **Yellow or Dijon mustard**
- 4 **thin sandwich buns**
- 2 **cups (loosely packed) baby spinach leaves**

Chicken Bok Choy *by Andrea Meyers,* **andreasrecipes.com**

4 tablespoons canola oil, divided

3 garlic cloves, minced

1 ½-inch knob fresh ginger, peeled and grated

3 boneless skinless chicken breasts, cut into ½-inch-thick strips

1 pound bok choy, trimmed, rinsed, and cut into 2-inch-long pieces

2 scallions, cut into 2-inch-long pieces

3 tablespoons low-sodium soy sauce

¼ cup chicken broth

A relative of cabbage, bok choy works well in both stir-fries and soups, and you can find it in both small and larger heads. The smaller heads are prized for their tenderness and flavor, and they cook pretty quickly, as in this chicken stir-fry. *Serves 4*

Heat 2 tablespoons of the oil in a wok or large skillet over high heat. Add the garlic and ginger and cook, stirring, until the edges of the garlic and ginger begin to brown, about 1 minute. Discard the garlic and ginger.

Add the chicken to the pan and cook, stirring, until the meat begins to turn white, 2 to 3 minutes. Transfer the chicken to a plate and cover.

Add the remaining 2 tablespoons oil and the bok choy to the pan, working in batches if needed. Stir-fry until the bok choy is hot but still firm, about 2 minutes. Add the scallions and cook until the vegetables are bright green but not yet tender, about 2 more minutes.

Return the chicken to the pan and add the soy sauce and chicken broth. Cook until the bok choy is crisp-tender and the chicken is fully cooked, 1 to 2 minutes. Serve immediately.

Chicken, Broccoli, & Brown Rice Dinner

by Jenny Flake, picky-palate.com

¼ cup extra-virgin olive oil

1 pound chicken sausages, thinly sliced

4 cups broccoli florets, steamed until fork-tender

4 cups cooked brown rice

¼ cup freshly grated Parmesan cheese

Salt and freshly ground black pepper

Speed up this dinner by cooking your rice the day before. You can use any variety of chicken sausage your family likes and add any of your favorite vegetables to this dish. Serve it with a side of green salad. *Serves 4*

Heat the oil in a large skillet over medium heat. Add the sausage slices and cook until browned, 2 to 3 minutes per side. Add the steamed broccoli, cooked rice, and cheese and cook, stirring, until hot, about 2 minutes. Season to taste with salt and pepper and serve.

Chicken Tinga *by Matt Armendariz,* mattbites.com

Chicken tinga is a quick and easy dish that's flavored with the unmistakable smokiness of chipotle peppers, which you can find in Latin markets. Because of its shredded preparation, it's naturally at home on top of crispy fried tostadas, tucked into a fluffy, warm flour tortilla, or even wrapped inside enchiladas. Make sure to top it with plenty of cool sour cream or Mexican crema and slices of avocado.
Serves 4

Place the chicken in a large pot. Add ¼ cup of the onions and the garlic and cover with water. Bring to a boil and cook until the chicken is fully cooked and its juices run clear, 20 to 30 minutes. Remove the chicken from the pot and discard the onions. Let the chicken cool and discard the skin and bones; use a fork to shred the chicken.

Heat the oil in a large skillet over medium heat. Add the remaining onions and cook, stirring, until golden-brown, 5 to 7 minutes.

Place the tomatoes in a blender or food processor and add the chipotle peppers, including the liquid in the can. Season to taste with salt and pepper and blend until smooth. Remove from the heat.

Place the blended tomato mixture in the large pot. Add the shredded chicken and cooked onions and cook over medium heat until the chicken is hot, about 5 minutes. Serve with the sour cream or crema, avocado slices, and tortillas.

6 chicken breast halves with skin and bones
6 medium yellow onions, thinly sliced, divided
1 garlic clove, minced
¼ cup canola or vegetable oil
6 medium tomatoes, peeled (see Make It Easy)
1 7-ounce can chipotle peppers in adobo sauce, undrained
   Salt and freshly ground black pepper
   Sour cream or Mexican crema
   Avocado slices
   Flour tortillas

MAKE IT EASY

Here's how to peel tomatoes: Remove the stems with a knife and cut an X in the bottom of each tomato. Boil a pot of water, use a slotted spoon to dip the tomatoes into the boiling water for a few seconds, then transfer the tomatoes to a bowl of ice water. Remove the cooled tomatoes and peel away the skin.

Chicken & Spinach Enchiladas
by Lori Lange, recipegirl.com

In Southern California, we see more Mexican food than you can ever imagine. It tends to end up on our dinner table quite often. These enchiladas have a creamy chicken filling and are topped with plenty of sauce and cheese. Serve them with guacamole, chopped fresh cilantro, chopped red onions—whatever accompaniments you like and have on hand. *Serves 4*

Preheat the oven to 350°F. Spray a 9×13-inch baking dish with nonstick cooking spray. Place ½ cup of the salsa and the enchilada sauce in a medium bowl and stir to combine; set aside.

Place the cream cheese in a microwave-safe medium bowl and heat in the microwave for 1 minute or until very soft. Add the spinach, chicken, and remaining 1½ cups salsa to the bowl and stir until blended.

Fill each tortilla with about ⅓ cup of the chicken mixture and roll up. Place the enchiladas, seam side down, in the prepared baking dish. Pour the enchilada sauce mixture evenly over the rolled tortillas and top with the cheese.

Bake until the cheese is melted and bubbling, about 30 minutes. Remove the enchiladas from the oven and let them rest for 5 minutes. Serve with desired toppings.

Nonstick cooking spray
2 cups salsa, divided
2 10-ounce cans enchilada sauce
¾ cup low-fat cream cheese
1 10-ounce package frozen chopped spinach, thawed and squeezed dry
2 cups chopped cooked chicken
8 8-inch flour tortillas
1 8-ounce package shredded Mexican four-cheese blend

MAKE IT EASY
Look for packaged cooked chicken tenders in the deli case at your local market. They're nice to use for this recipe when you're in a big hurry to get dinner on the table.

Chicken & Turkey

Hainanese Chicken Salad *by Marc Matsumoto,* norecipes.com

½ seedless cucumber, julienned

1 small onion, thinly sliced

2 quarts water

2 tablespoons plus 1½ teaspoons kosher salt, divided

3 boneless skinless chicken breasts

1 1-inch knob fresh ginger, peeled and finely grated (about 2 tablespoons)

2 scallions, finely minced

3 tablespoons vegetable oil

1 tablespoon toasted sesame oil

⅛ teaspoon freshly ground white pepper

1 tablespoon fresh lemon juice

⅓ pound arugula, washed and dried

Fresh cilantro leaves, for garnish

Hainanese chicken originated on the southern Chinese island of Hainan. It normally includes a whole chicken that's gently poached in water, making the meat both tender and moist. The poaching liquid is then used to cook the rice, and the chicken and rice are served with a pungent ginger-scallion sauce. This healthier take on the classic is easier to prepare and lower in fat and carbs.

Here, the chicken breast is shredded, allowing it to absorb all the flavors from the ginger-scallion oil, while the crisp bed of cucumber and tamed onion provides a wonderful cool contrast to the tender meat. Serving the salad on a lofty bed of arugula gives this dish a rich, peppery taste while providing enough bulk to make it a filling meal. Putting the cucumber and onion in ice water makes them crisp and sweetens the onion. *Serves 4*

Place the cucumber and onion in a large bowl filled with ice water.

Bring the 2 quarts water and 2 tablespoons of the kosher salt to a boil in a large heavy pot with a lid (such as a Dutch oven). Add the chicken breasts, cover, and remove from the heat. Let the chicken poach until cooked, about 30 minutes. Remove the cooked chicken and shred it into a medium bowl.

To make the ginger-scallion sauce, place the ginger, scallions, vegetable oil, sesame oil, remaining 1½ teaspoons kosher salt, and the white pepper in a small bowl and stir to combine.

Add 3 tablespoons of the ginger-scallion sauce to the shredded chicken and toss to coat.

Thoroughly drain the onion and cucumber. Add the remaining ginger-scallion sauce and the lemon juice to the onion and cucumber and toss to coat.

To serve, place a layer of arugula and a layer of the prepared onion and cucumber on each plate. Top with a mound of chicken, then scatter a few cilantro leaves on top of the salad.

Chicken with Sun-Dried Tomatoes, Shallots, & Thyme
by Andrea Meyers, **andreasrecipes.com**

Sun-dried tomatoes add robust flavor to this simple dish, which you can alter by adjusting the amount of tomatoes to your taste. If you prefer a little less sauce, reduce the amount of wine to $\frac{1}{2}$ cup. Serve with seasonal roasted or sautéed vegetables. *Serves 4*

Heat the oil in a large skillet over medium heat. Add the shallots, 2 of the thyme sprigs, and the garlic and cook, stirring, until the shallots are translucent, about 3 minutes.

Add the chicken strips to the skillet and cook until golden-brown, about 5 minutes per side. Add the sun-dried tomatoes and stir. Add the wine, sea salt, pepper, and the remaining 2 thyme sprigs. Cook until the wine reduces and thickens slightly, 3 to 5 minutes. Remove the thyme sprigs and serve immediately.

- ¼ cup light olive oil
- 12 shallots, quartered lengthwise
- 4 sprigs fresh thyme, divided
- 3 garlic cloves, minced
- 4 boneless skinless chicken breasts, cut into strips 2 inches wide by 4 inches long
- 6 sun-dried tomatoes in oil, chopped
- ⅔ cup dry white wine
- ½ teaspoon sea salt
- ¼ teaspoon freshly ground black pepper

Jenny Flake, picky-palate.com

Jenny Flake is the author of the family-friendly, home-style cooking and recipe blog Picky Palate (picky-palate.com). She is a proud home cook, the on-the-go mom of two little boys, and the wife of her high school sweetheart. Before Jenny started writing Picky Palate, she was a registered dental hygienist, a certified Pilates instructor, and a participant in cooking contests all over the country. She's been on Food Network's *Build a Better Burger*, *The Ultimate Recipe Showdown*, the National Chicken Cook-Off, and the Pillsbury Bake-Off. Picky Palate has been featured on sites such as Saveur.com and BettyCrocker.com. Creating original recipes and capturing food photography are Jenny's new passions and she loves sharing her journey with her readers.

More About Jenny

What do you always have in your shopping cart?
Fresh produce! Garlic, onions, cilantro, parsley, bananas, strawberries, and apples.

What's your go-to weeknight dinner?
Homemade spaghetti and meatballs, by far my family's favorite.

What's your favorite kitchen tool?
Absolutely my rubber spatulas; I use them daily.

Is there anything you just can't eat?
I'll try anything once. However, I'm not a fan of oysters.

Chicken, Roasted Red Pepper, & Spinach Quinoa *by Jenny Flake*, picky-palate.com

Quinoa is a great substitute for rice. It takes only about 10 minutes to cook, which makes for quick weeknight dinners. Find a jar of roasted red peppers in your grocery store to save time. Shred your rotisserie chicken ahead of time and dinner is a breeze! *Serves 4*

Place the cheese, kosher salt, garlic salt, and black pepper in a small bowl and toss to combine; set aside. Prepare the quinoa according to the package instructions.

While the quinoa cooks, heat the oil in a large skillet over medium heat. Add the onion and spinach and cook, stirring, until the onion is softened and the spinach is wilted, about 5 minutes. Add the garlic, stir, and cook for 1 minute. Add the roasted red peppers and shredded chicken.

Add the cooked quinoa to the cheese mixture, stir to combine, then add the mixture to the skillet. Reduce the heat to low and cook until the chicken is warm, 3 to 5 minutes. Serve immediately.

⅓ cup crumbled feta cheese
½ teaspoon kosher salt
¼ teaspoon garlic salt
¼ teaspoon freshly ground black pepper
1 cup quinoa
3 tablespoons extra-virgin olive oil
½ cup finely chopped onion
4 cups (loosely packed) chopped baby spinach leaves
2 tablespoons minced garlic
2 cups chopped roasted red peppers
2 cups shredded rotisserie chicken

Peruvian Grilled Chicken *by Andrea Meyers,* andreasrecipes.com

⅓ cup low-sodium soy sauce

2 tablespoons fresh lime juice

5 garlic cloves, minced

2 teaspoons ground cumin

1 teaspoon paprika

½ teaspoon dried oregano

½ teaspoon freshly ground black
   pepper

1 tablespoon canola oil, plus
   additional for brushing grill

4 boneless skinless chicken
   breasts, trimmed and pounded
   to a ½-inch thickness between
   two sheets of plastic wrap

1 lime, cut into wedges

This easy chicken dish gets its flavor from a long stay in the spicy soy-lime marinade, and the boneless skinless chicken breasts grill quickly. To complete the meal, grill some vegetables to go with it, or slice the meat and use it as a salad topper or in whole grain tortilla wraps. *Serves 4*

Place the soy sauce, lime juice, garlic, cumin, paprika, oregano, pepper, and oil in a large bowl and whisk to combine. Add the chicken breasts, toss gently, cover, and marinate in the refrigerator for 8 to 24 hours.

Brush the grill rack with oil and prepare the grill to medium-high. Discard the marinade and pat the chicken dry. Grill the chicken until it is browned and the center is no longer pink, 4 to 5 minutes per side.

Remove the chicken from the grill and let it rest for 1 to 2 minutes. Squeeze lime juice over the chicken and serve.

Andrea Meyers, andreasrecipes.com

Andrea Meyers blogs about cooking, edible gardening, and her four hungry guys at Andrea's Recipes (andreasrecipes.com). She has been featured in the *Washington Post* and on Café Mom and Houzz.com. Andrea grew up on her family's good Southern fare and learned to love other cuisines during her years working abroad. She spent eight years teaching in Saudi Arabia, Colombia, and Saipan and has traveled in the Pacific Rim, Asia, Australia, South America, Europe, and the Middle East, sampling local foods and collecting recipes along the way. Andrea lives with her family in Northern Virginia, where they are turning their backyard into an edible landscape.

More About Andrea

What do you always have in your shopping cart?
We keep a constant supply of yogurt and olive oil.

What's your go-to weeknight dinner?
Our family enjoys panini as a weekly meal because we can all choose our own favorite sandwich fillings.

What's your favorite kitchen tool?
I use my santoku knife every single day, because the blade works so well with the kind of food we prepare.

Is there anything you just can't eat?
There are a few things I can't eat, but liver is at the top of the list.

Smoked Turkey & Artichoke Panini

by Sara Wells, ourbestbites.com

Tangy artichokes, smoked turkey, and smooth, melted cheese come together in this quick grilled sandwich. The fresh spinach and tomatoes bring a little balance to the meal, and the flavored mayonnaise takes it to another level. *Serves 4*

Place the mayonnaise, garlic, lemon juice, and basil in a small bowl and whisk to combine. Spread the flavored mayonnaise on one side of each bread slice. Layer the turkey on 4 bread slices and top each with spinach, cheese, artichokes, and tomatoes. Cover with the remaining bread slices, with the mayonnaise side facing down. Lightly brush both sides of each sandwich with olive oil.

Heat a panini press or panini pan, or prepare the grill to medium-high. Place the sandwiches in the press or pan or on the grill. Cover and cook until the cheese is melted and the bread is golden-brown, about 5 minutes if using a panini press, or 5 minutes per side if using a grill. Serve immediately.

¾ cup mayonnaise

1 garlic clove, minced

1½ teaspoons fresh lemon juice

1 teaspoon dried basil

8 slices rustic sourdough bread

¾ pound thinly sliced smoked deli turkey

2 cups (loosely packed) spinach leaves

8 slices Swiss cheese

1 7-ounce jar marinated artichoke hearts, drained and halved lengthwise

2 plum tomatoes, sliced
Extra-virgin olive oil

MAKE IT EASY

For more intense flavor, make the flavored mayonnaise a couple of days ahead of time. It will keep for 1 week when stored in an airtight container in the fridge.

"With three little ones at home, I rely on recipes that are simple but satisfying. It's the only way to keep things balanced throughout the week."

—*Sara Wells*

TWO

Beef & Lamb

Grilled Filet Mignon & Heirloom Tomato Salad *by Laura Levy,* laurasbestrecipes.com

This recipe is a favorite in my house. I like using organic or grass-fed beef because it's healthier and more environmentally conscious, and I leave the steaks out for at least half an hour before grilling so they are at room temperature; the meat cooks more quickly and evenly when it's closer to the temperature of the grill. *Serves 4*

Place the tomatoes, oil, basil, thyme, sea salt, and pepper in a large bowl, tossing gently to coat. Set aside.

Brush the grill rack with oil and prepare the grill to medium-high. Season the steaks with sea salt and pepper. Grill the steaks to desired doneness, about 5 minutes per side for medium-rare. Remove the steaks from the heat and let them rest for 5 to 7 minutes.

Season the steaks to taste with sea salt and pepper, and serve immediately with the heirloom tomato salad. Add the cheese to the salad before serving, if desired.

4 large heirloom tomatoes, cored and cut into ¼-inch-thick slices
¼ cup olive oil, plus additional for brushing grill
¼ cup chopped fresh basil leaves
¼ cup chopped fresh thyme
½ teaspoon sea salt, plus additional for seasoning
½ teaspoon freshly ground black pepper, plus additional for seasoning
4 6-ounce filet mignon steaks, 1½ inches thick
Thinly sliced Pecorino Romano cheese (optional)

MAKE IT EASY
For a less expensive option, try this recipe with a sirloin steak or rib-eye. Test doneness by pressing the top of the steak: a medium-rare steak will give a little to the touch but won't retain an impression of your finger. Or you can test the temperature with an instant meat thermometer; medium-rare is about 140°F.

Skirt Steak Fajitas *by Catherine McCord,* weelicious.com

¼ cup (packed) fresh cilantro leaves
¼ cup fresh lime juice
¼ cup soy sauce
¼ cup tequila
2 garlic cloves
3 tablespoons olive oil, divided
1 pound skirt steak
1 large yellow onion, thinly sliced
1 large red bell pepper, stemmed, seeded, and thinly sliced
Flour or corn tortillas
Sour cream (optional)
Guacamole (optional)

Meat can be quite expensive, especially when you're on a budget. I like to make these skirt steak fajitas when I'm feeding a crowd, because a little goes a long way. Skirt steak has a juicy, meaty flavor that only becomes more tender from the tequila and cilantro marinade. With the addition of the sautéed peppers and onions and other accompaniments, it becomes not only a fast recipe to prepare but also something that's a lot of fun for those you're serving! *Serves 4*

Place the cilantro, lime juice, soy sauce, tequila, garlic, and 2 tablespoons of the oil in a blender or food processor and blend or process until combined. Place the steak in a large resealable plastic bag and add the marinade (you may need to cut the skirt steak into several large slabs). Marinate in the refrigerator for 4 to 24 hours.

Heat the remaining 1 tablespoon oil in a large skillet over medium-high heat. Remove the steak from the marinade, discarding the marinade. Add the meat to the skillet and cook until browned, about 2 minutes per side. Transfer the steak to a cutting board and let it rest for 5 to 10 minutes.

While the steak is resting, reduce the heat under the skillet to medium and add the onion and pepper. Cook until the vegetables begin to become tender and the edges are golden, 4 to 5 minutes. Remove from the heat.

Slice the steak into thin strips. Serve with the vegetables, tortillas, and sour cream and guacamole, if desired.

MAKE IT EASY
After preparing the marinade, chop the onion and pepper and place them in a resealable plastic bag in the fridge, so you can just toss them in the pan after cooking the meat later in the day or the next day. To soften a stack of tortillas, place them in a completely sealed foil pouch and bake in a 350°F oven until they're warm and soft, about 10 minutes.

Korean Barbecue Beef Skewers

by Kate Jones, ourbestbites.com

This thinly sliced steak cooks to tender, glazed perfection after just a few minutes on the grill. If using bamboo skewers, be sure to soak them in water for 30 minutes to an hour before grilling to prevent them from burning. You can whisk the marinade ingredients together first thing in the morning and combine them with the steak, allowing the meat to become tender and flavorful. Serve this with a green salad or some steamed vegetables. *Serves 4*

Place the steak in a large resealable plastic bag. Place the pear juice, soy sauce, scallions, brown sugar, garlic, ginger, Sriracha sauce, and sesame oil in a medium bowl and whisk to combine. Add the marinade to the bag and knead gently to combine. Marinate in the refrigerator for 4 to 8 hours or at room temperature for 1 hour.

Prepare the grill to medium-high. Thread the steak onto skewers (see Head-note if using bamboo skewers) and grill to desired doneness, 3 to 5 minutes per side for medium. Serve immediately.

1 1-pound flank or sirloin steak, cut against the grain into ¼-inch-thick slices
½ cup pear juice
⅓ cup low-sodium soy sauce
¼ cup chopped scallions
2 tablespoons brown sugar
2 tablespoons minced garlic
1 teaspoon grated fresh ginger
1 teaspoon Sriracha sauce
1½ teaspoons toasted sesame oil

MAKE IT EASY
You can buy a 4-ounce bottle of pear juice in the baby food aisle of the supermarket. It's inexpensive and just the amount you need for this recipe.

Grilled Steaks with Onions, Roasted Potatoes, & Bacon

by Shauna James Ahern and Daniel Ahern, **glutenfreegirl.com**

- 2 pounds Red Bliss potatoes, halved
- 4 10-ounce rib-eye steaks, 2 inches thick
- 2 tablespoons olive oil, divided
  Salt and freshly ground black pepper
- 2 large yellow onions, cut into ½-inch-thick slices
- 8 slices thick-cut bacon, cut into 1-inch pieces
- 2 teaspoons chopped fresh rosemary

During the summer, when it's barbecuing season, this is the perfect quick dish. The smoky onions smell amazing. This steak is almost like being out camping. Sautéed bacon and potatoes are just a slice of heaven. This is a whole lot of love in one dish. *Serves 4*

Place the potatoes in a large pot of cold salted water over medium-high heat. Bring the water to a boil and cook the potatoes until they are easily pierced with a fork, about 15 minutes. Drain the potatoes and set aside.

Preheat the oven to 200°F. Prepare the grill to medium-high. Rub each side of each steak with ½ teaspoon of the oil and season with salt and pepper. Grill the steaks until the bottoms are charred, about 3 minutes. Rotate the steaks 90 degrees and cook for 2 more minutes. Turn over the steaks and cook to just before desired doneness, about 5 more minutes for medium-rare.

While the steaks are cooking, place the onions on the hottest part of the grill and cook until lightly charred, about 3 minutes per side.

Remove the steaks and onions from the grill. Set the grilled onions aside. Place an inverted saucer on a large plate. Drape the steaks over the saucer to let them rest. Transfer the plate to the oven.

Heat the remaining 2 teaspoons oil in a large skillet over medium-high heat. Add the bacon pieces and cook until crisp. Remove the bacon from the skillet, reserving the bacon fat and oil in the pan. Reduce the heat to medium and add the blanched potatoes to the skillet, cut side down. Cook until the potatoes are browned, about 2 minutes per side. Remove from the heat, season to taste with salt and pepper, and toss with the rosemary. Serve the steaks immediately, topped with the grilled onions and bacon and with the potatoes alongside.

Grilled Rib-Eye with Grilled Romaine & Avocado Salad *by Laura Levy,* laurasbestrecipes.com

This dish is easily adapted to different flavors: add adobo or a tablespoon of diced chipotle to the vinaigrette and serve with cayenne-spiced corn on the cob for a Southwestern theme, or try adding anchovies for a classic Caesar salad vibe.

You can make the vinaigrette ahead to save time. It will keep in the refrigerator for several days. As always, I recommend using organic ingredients. *Serves 4*

Pat the steak dry and season to taste with sea salt and pepper.

Brush the grill rack with oil and prepare the grill to high.

Place the cheese, lemon juice, garlic, shallots, mustard, vinegar, and 1 cup oil in a medium bowl, whisking to combine. Set the vinaigrette aside.

Grill the steak to desired doneness, 5 to 7 minutes per side for medium-rare. Remove the steak from the heat and let it rest for 10 minutes.

Reduce the grill heat to medium. Brush the cut sides of the avocados with oil and season to taste with sea salt and pepper. Grill the avocados, cut side down, for 2 to 3 minutes. Remove from the heat and cut the avocado halves into slices, gently removing the slices from the peel with a spoon.

Lightly brush the cut sides of the romaine lettuce with oil. Grill the lettuce until lightly seared, 30 seconds to 1 minute. Transfer the lettuce to a large bowl, add the vinaigrette and avocado, and toss gently.

Using a sharp knife, cut the rib-eye into very thin strips. Serve with the romaine and avocado salad.

1 1-pound rib-eye steak, 1½ inches thick
  Sea salt and freshly ground black pepper
1 cup extra-virgin olive oil, plus additional for brushing grill, avocados, and lettuce
¼ cup freshly grated Parmesan cheese
3 tablespoons fresh Meyer lemon juice or regular fresh lemon juice
2 teaspoons minced garlic
3 shallots, minced
1 tablespoon Dijon mustard
1 tablespoon red wine vinegar
2 ripe but firm Hass avocados, unpeeled, halved and pitted
1 large romaine heart, base and top trimmed, quartered lengthwise, and rinsed

Dressed-Up Sloppy Joes *by Kate Jones,* ourbestbites.com

- 3 tablespoons olive oil
- 1 medium onion, chopped
- ½ green bell pepper, stemmed, seeded, and chopped
- 3 garlic cloves, minced
- 1 pound lean ground beef
  Seasoned salt
- ¾ cup ketchup
- 3 tablespoons plus 1 teaspoon brown sugar
- 1½ teaspoons red wine vinegar
- 1 teaspoon yellow mustard
- 1 teaspoon Worcestershire sauce
- 3 tablespoons tomato paste
- ⅓ cup water
  Freshly ground black pepper
- 4 to 6 high-quality sandwich or hamburger buns

Sloppy joes may have a bad cafeteria reputation, but in this recipe, ground beef is simmered in a savory tomato-based sauce and seasoned to perfection. Serve it on a high-quality sandwich roll and it's something picky eaters and foodies can finally agree on. To avoid wasting a whole can of tomato paste, look for the squeeze tubes sometimes found in the pasta sauce aisle in the supermarket. *Serves 4 to 6*

Heat the oil in a large saucepan over medium-high heat. Add the onion, bell pepper, garlic, and ground beef. Cook, breaking up the meat with a spatula, until the beef is browned and fully cooked, about 5 minutes. Season to taste with seasoned salt. Add the ketchup, brown sugar, vinegar, mustard, and Worcestershire sauce and stir. Add the tomato paste and water and stir well to combine. Season to taste with black pepper. Cover, reduce the heat to low, and simmer until thickened, stirring occasionally and adding more water if needed, about 30 minutes. Serve on the buns.

MAKE IT EASY
You can freeze the hamburger and sauce mixture for up to 3 months. When you're ready to serve it, just put it in a slow cooker and cook on low for 4 hours.

Julie Van Rosendaal, dinnerwithjulie.com

Julie is a freelance food writer and the author of the best-selling cookbooks *One Smart Cookie*, *Starting Out*, and *Grazing*. She is the food editor of *Parents Canada* magazine and the food and nutrition columnist on the *Calgary Eyeopener* on CBC Radio One. Julie is a regular on local morning shows and cohosts *It's Just Food* on the Viva television network. She teaches at cooking schools across Canada. She also writes and takes photographs for her popular food blog, Dinner with Julie (dinnerwithjulie.com), which documents real life in her home kitchen. Julie lives in Calgary, Alberta, with her musician husband, Mike; four-year-old son, Willem; and big black dog, Lou.

More About Julie

What do you always have in your shopping cart?

Besides milk, butter, and eggs—dark red apples (my four-year-old goes through several a day), kale (I'm addicted to it in chip form), cheese, locally made yogurt, barley, oats, dried lentils, chickpeas, greens, nuts, garlic, maple syrup, and canola oil. Wow, that makes me sound really healthy, doesn't it?

What's your go-to weeknight dinner?

The boys will always eat spaghetti and meatballs—there's a fantastic sausage producer blocks from our house, so we buy their Italian sausages and squeeze them out of the casings at meatball-size intervals, brown them, then simmer them in tomato sauce as the pasta cooks. Fried rice is also common—it's a great way to use up whatever is left over in the fridge.

What's your favorite kitchen tool?

My favorite kitchen tools are from my grandma's house—her metal nesting measuring cups and well-used pastry blender. I'm not a very gadgety person, but I love my slow cooker, my handheld immersion blender (great for pureeing soups right in the pot—I hate having to transfer it in batches to a blender, and we still have soup splatters on our ceiling from one particular mishap), and my ice-cream maker.

Is there anything you just can't eat?

Black licorice! And oysters. No can do.

Curried Lamb & Lentils

by Julie Van Rosendaal, dinnerwithjulie.com

Flavorful lamb leg or shoulder requires a long, slow cooking time to break down tough connective tissues; cooking the lamb along with dried lentils, which don't require soaking, infuses the legumes with the flavor of the lamb. If you like, stir one or two chopped carrots, a handful of halved new potatoes, or a cup of cauliflower florets into the pot halfway through the cooking time. Serve this with rice or fresh naan for a hearty dinner. *Serves 6*

Heat the oil in a large heavy skillet over medium-high heat. Pat the lamb dry and, working in batches, cook the lamb until browned, about 5 minutes per side. Transfer the browned meat to a slow cooker.

If needed, add another tablespoon of oil to the pan and add the onion, cooking until it softens and begins to turn golden, about 5 minutes. Add the jalapeño and garlic and cook for 1 minute. Transfer the mixture to the slow cooker. Pour the water into the skillet and swirl, scraping up any browned bits from the bottom of the pan; transfer the liquid to the slow cooker. Add the tomatoes, lentils, and curry paste or powder to the slow cooker and cover.

Cook on low until the lamb is very tender, 6 to 8 hours. Season to taste with salt and pepper and serve hot over hot cooked rice or with fresh naan.

1 tablespoon canola or olive oil, plus 1 tablespoon additional if needed
1 pound lamb shoulder or boneless leg, cut into 1-inch pieces
1 onion, chopped
1 jalapeño chile, seeded and chopped (optional)
2 garlic cloves, chopped
1 cup water
1 28-ounce can whole plum tomatoes, undrained
1 cup dried green lentils
1 tablespoon curry paste or powder
Salt and freshly ground black pepper
Hot cooked rice or fresh naan

Steak & Goat Cheese Quesadillas with Corn & Tomato Relish *by Jenny Flake,* picky-palate.com

4 warm steaks, grilled or seared and cut into ½-inch pieces

¼ teaspoon garlic salt

¼ teaspoon sea salt, plus additional for seasoning steak

¼ teaspoon freshly ground black pepper, plus additional for seasoning steak

1 tablespoon extra-virgin olive oil

2½ cups corn kernels

1 cup quartered grape tomatoes

¼ cup (loosely packed) fresh cilantro leaves, finely chopped

2 to 3 tablespoons unsalted butter, softened

8 8-inch flour tortillas

½ cup crumbled goat cheese

Use your favorite cut of steak for this recipe and cook it up however you like. Be sure to cut the steak into small pieces for the quesadilla. You can substitute your family's favorite cheese for the goat cheese.
Serves 6 to 8

Season the cooked, warm steak pieces with the garlic salt and season to taste with salt and pepper.

Heat the oil in a large skillet over medium heat. Add the corn, tomatoes, cilantro, ¼ teaspoon salt, and ¼ teaspoon pepper. Cook until warm and fragrant, about 5 minutes, and set the corn and tomato relish aside.

Lightly spread the butter on one side of each tortilla. Place 1 tortilla, buttered side down, in another large skillet over medium heat. Add 1 tablespoon of the cheese to half of the tortilla, then add a few pieces of chopped steak. Using a spatula, fold over the other side of the tortilla and cook until golden-brown and crisp, about 2 minutes per side. Transfer the quesadilla to a plate and repeat with the remaining ingredients. Serve immediately, topping each quesadilla with the corn and tomato relish.

Harvest Beef Casserole *by Christy Jordan,* southernplate.com

My husband's Granny Jordan was known near and far as a gracious Southern lady and wonderful host. She loved to cook and casseroles were her specialty. This quick and filling casserole is one for which I am especially grateful. Even my pickiest eater loves it! *Serves 4*

Preheat the oven to 350°F. Prepare the pasta according to the package instructions; rinse and drain.

Place the cooked pasta, soup, cheese, salt, ground beef, and vegetables in a large bowl and stir to combine. Transfer the mixture to a greased 2-quart casserole dish. Cover and bake until bubbly, about 30 minutes. Uncover the casserole, top with the french-fried onions, and bake 5 more minutes. Serve hot.

- **2 cups macaroni**
- **1 10.75-ounce can cream of mushroom soup**
- **1 cup shredded Cheddar cheese**
- **1 teaspoon seasoned salt**
- **1 pound lean ground beef, cooked and drained**
- **2 cups frozen mixed vegetables (peas, carrots, and corn)**
- **1 6-ounce can french-fried onions**

Grilled Flank Steak with Chimichurri Sauce

by Matt Armendariz, **mattbites.com**

I love to serve this dish by slicing off a piece of flank steak and dipping it into the chimichurri sauce, but you can drizzle the sauce over the flank and enjoy it that way, too!

If you have time, make a bigger batch of chimichurri sauce and use some to marinate the meat for extra flavor. *Serves 6*

Place the vinegar and garlic in a medium bowl, stir to combine, and let the mixture rest for 15 minutes. Add the oil, parsley, cilantro, and red pepper flakes and stir. Season the chimichurri sauce to taste with salt.

Pat the steak dry and generously season it with salt and black pepper. Prepare the grill to medium-high and brush the steak lightly with oil. Grill the steak to desired doneness, 3 to 4 minutes per side for medium-rare. Serve immediately with the chimichurri sauce.

¼ cup red wine vinegar
2 garlic cloves, finely chopped
¾ cup extra-virgin olive oil, plus additional for brushing steaks
¼ cup chopped fresh Italian parsley
¼ cup chopped fresh cilantro leaves
¼ teaspoon red pepper flakes
  Kosher salt or sea salt
1 1½-pound flank steak
  Freshly ground black pepper

MAKE IT EASY
If you don't feel like grilling, you can sear the flank steak instead. Just heat 1 to 2 tablespoons vegetable oil in a large pan until the oil is lightly smoking; add the steak and cook until browned, 3 to 5 minutes per side, depending on the thickness. Serve with some crusty bread.

Beef & Lamb

87

"During the week, this recipe hits the spot—there's nothing easier than flank steak when it comes to cooking. The chimichurri can be made ahead of time, too."

—Matt Armendariz

Garlic Burgers with Homemade Barbecue Sauce *by Todd Porter and Diane Cu,* whiteonricecouple.com

FOR SAUCE:

- 3 tablespoons vegetable oil
- 1 small onion, finely chopped
- 3 garlic cloves, minced
- 1 cup water
- ½ cup diced fresh pineapple
- ½ cup tomato sauce
- ½ cup ketchup
- ½ cup apple cider vinegar
- 3 tablespoons Worcestershire sauce
- 1½ tablespoons fresh lemon juice
- 3 tablespoons brown sugar
- 2 tablespoons molasses
- 1 tablespoon yellow mustard
- 1 tablespoon mustard powder
- 1 teaspoon Sriracha sauce
- 1 teaspoon soy sauce
  Freshly ground black pepper

FOR BURGERS:

- 2 pounds lean ground beef
- 2 garlic cloves, crushed
  Freshly ground black pepper
  Olive oil, for brushing grill
- 6 hamburger buns
- 1 teaspoon sea salt

Packed with garlicky flavor, these burgers will be a hit with your family. You can use store-bought sauce, but dressing them with this fresh, easy-to-make barbecue sauce makes the garlic burgers truly outstanding. Don't be intimidated by the long list of ingredients—the sauce is worth it, and it keeps for a couple of weeks. *Serves 6*

For Sauce: Heat the vegetable oil in a large saucepan over medium heat. Add the onion and garlic and cook until softened, about 4 minutes. Add the water, pineapple, tomato sauce, ketchup, vinegar, Worcestershire sauce, lemon juice, brown sugar, molasses, yellow mustard, mustard powder, Sriracha sauce, soy sauce, and pepper. Stir and bring to a simmer, about 15 minutes.

Remove the barbecue sauce from the heat and let it cool, about 30 minutes. Set aside; if making ahead, store the sauce in an airtight container in the fridge. (For a finer texture, puree the cooled sauce in a blender, then press it through a fine-mesh strainer over a medium bowl.)

For Burgers: Place the ground beef, garlic, and pepper to taste in a large bowl and use your hands to combine. Form the beef mixture into 6 patties. Brush the grill rack or grill pan with olive oil and prepare the grill or grill pan to medium-high. Grill the buns, cut side down, until golden, about 2 minutes, and remove from the heat.

Season both sides of each beef patty with sea salt and grill to desired doneness, about 3 minutes per side for medium. Place a burger and barbecue sauce on each bun bottom; add other toppings as desired, add the bun top, and serve.

MAKE IT EASY
The barbecue sauce can be made ahead and stored in an airtight container in the fridge; it will keep for 2 to 3 weeks. The beef patties can be made up to 1 day ahead; store them covered in the fridge.

Todd Porter and Diane Cu,

whiteonricecouple.com

Diane Cu and Todd Porter are Southern California–based photographers, food writers, and cooking instructors. By day, they stay busy in their photography and multimedia studio, contribute to *Edible Los Angeles* magazine and Zester Daily, teach barbecue and Asian cooking classes, and lead Vietnamese culinary tours. By night, they share their life of food, gardening, travel, and photography with the readers of their blog, White On Rice Couple (whiteonricecouple.com). When not on assignment or in the studio, kitchen, or garden, Diane and Todd are out exploring local and global food cultures.

More About Diane and Todd

What do you always have in your shopping cart?
Garlic, ginger, shallots, Plugrá butter, grapeseed oil, fish sauce, and Maggi seasoning sauce.

What's your go-to weeknight dinner?
Our go-to weeknight dinner is fresh rice paper spring rolls; bread, cheese, and charcuterie; and lots of wine and cocktails.

What's your favorite kitchen tool?
A good chef's knife and our mortar and pestle.

Is there anything you just can't eat?
Diane can't eat snake, and Todd can't eat fetal duck eggs.

Beef Tacos *by Marc Matsumoto,* norecipes.com

2 teaspoons vegetable oil
½ medium onion, chopped
2 garlic cloves, minced
1 pound lean ground beef
2 tablespoons chili powder
1 teaspoon kosher salt
½ teaspoon sugar
12 6-inch corn tortillas
   Salsa verde or pico de gallo
   Chopped fresh cilantro leaves
   Lime wedges

These beef tacos are the kind of weeknight meal I prepare when I come home after a long day of meetings only to find the fridge devoid of anything even remotely inspirational. At times like this, I'm almost tempted by the phone and a takeout menu that someone surreptitiously slipped under my door. Thankfully, standbys like these beef tacos are at the ready to save me from almost certain heartburn.

This recipe is really easy—just prepare the components and let everyone build his or her own taco. *Serves 4*

Heat the oil in a large skillet over medium-high heat. Add the onion and garlic and cook, stirring, until the onion is just translucent, about 2 minutes. Add the ground beef, chili powder, kosher salt, and sugar; stir-fry until the beef is browned and there is no liquid in the pan, 4 to 5 minutes. Remove from the heat.

Wrap the tortillas in damp paper towels and heat for 30 seconds in the microwave. Serve immediately with the prepared beef, salsa verde or pico de gallo, cilantro, and lime wedges.

Pizza Rolls *by Christy Jordan,* southernplate.com

This recipe was very popular at our house when my siblings and I were teenagers. With all of us heading out in different directions, my mother often made a batch or two of pizza rolls on the weekend so everyone could grab a meal on the run. Today, I make them whenever I have to go out of town, and I know my husband and kids will be happy. *Serves 6*

Place the ground beef, bell pepper, and onion in a large nonstick skillet over medium heat. Cook, stirring to break up the meat, until the beef is no longer pink, about 7 minutes. Add the pizza sauce and stir. Add ½ cup of the cheese, stir, and remove from the heat. Divide the prepared meat mixture among the buns or rolls. Top the pizza rolls with the remaining 1 cup cheese and serve immediately.

1 **pound lean ground beef**
½ **cup chopped green bell pepper**
½ **cup chopped onion**
1 **14-ounce jar pizza sauce**
1½ **cups shredded mozzarella cheese, divided**
6 **hot dog buns or sandwich rolls**

Grilled Lamb Chop Lollipops with Spinach & Tomato Couscous Salad

by Laura Levy, laurasbestrecipes.com

Ask the butcher to french the lamb (this means removing the fat and meat that connect the rib bones) and to cut it into chops for you. I like to start this recipe with my lamb at room temperature, so it grills more quickly and evenly. *Serves 4*

Season the lamb chops with salt and pepper.

Brush the grill rack with oil and prepare the grill to high. Place the lamb chops on the grill, cover, and cook until charred and to desired doneness, about 4 minutes per side for medium-rare. Transfer the chops to a plate, cover to keep warm, and set aside.

Preheat the oven to 400°F. Prepare the couscous according to the package instructions. Drain the couscous and transfer to a large serving bowl.

Place the tomatoes, cut side up, on a baking sheet, drizzle with 2 tablespoons of the oil, and season to taste with salt and pepper. Roast the tomatoes in the oven until they begin to collapse but are still slightly firm, about 8 minutes.

While the tomatoes roast, heat the remaining 2 tablespoons olive oil in a medium skillet over medium-high heat. Add the garlic and cook, stirring, until fragrant, about 1 minute. Add the spinach and cook, stirring, until wilted, about 2 minutes.

Add the roasted tomatoes and spinach to the couscous and toss gently. Season to taste with salt and pepper.

To serve, spoon the spinach and tomato couscous salad on each plate and sprinkle with some of the cheese. Place 3 to 4 lamb chops on each plate and season to taste with pepper. Serve immediately.

3 racks of lamb, frenched and cut into 1½-inch-thick chops
Salt and freshly ground black pepper
Olive oil, for brushing grill and drizzling tomatoes
1 cup dry couscous
½ pound ripe heirloom cherry or grape tomatoes, halved
4 tablespoons extra-virgin olive oil, divided
3 garlic cloves, diced
5 cups (loosely packed) spinach leaves
¼ cup crumbled goat cheese

MAKE IT EASY

To save a few steps, you can add the uncooked tomatoes and spinach to the cooked couscous instead of cooking them first. Drizzle with a little bit of olive oil, season to taste with salt and pepper, and serve with the lamb chops.

Beef & Lamb

95

Italian Burger *by Sara Wells,* **ourbestbites.com**

½ **pound Italian turkey sausage,**
  casings removed
½ **pound lean ground beef**
½ **teaspoon kosher salt**
¼ **teaspoon freshly ground black**
  pepper
4 **slices fresh mozzarella cheese**
4 **hamburger buns or Italian rolls**
1 **cup marinara sauce**

The Italian turkey sausage in this burger packs tremendous flavor and saves you time because you don't need to measure out spices. Topped with fresh mozzarella cheese and marinara sauce, the burger is like a giant meatball sandwich! *Serves 4*

Prepare the grill or grill pan to medium-high. Place the turkey sausage and ground sirloin in a medium bowl. Add the kosher salt and pepper and combine, using your hands.

Form the meat into four ½-inch-thick patties. Grill until the burgers are plump and grill marked, about 3 minutes, then turn over and cook for 2 more minutes. Place 1 slice of cheese on each burger and place the buns or rolls, cut side down, on the grill. Cook the burgers for 1 to 2 more minutes, until the cheese is melted and the internal temperature of the meat is 165°F. Remove the burgers from the heat. Remove the buns from the heat when they are lightly toasted.

Spread each bun bottom with 1 to 2 tablespoons marinara sauce. Top each bun bottom with a burger, add 1 to 2 more tablespoons marinara sauce to each, then cover with the bun tops. Serve immediately.

One-Skillet Chili Bake *by Christy Jordan,* **southernplate.com**

During football season, the men in my life love snacking on this recipe while watching the game, but it's also my favorite go-to for a meal-in-one supper. The kids love that I let them forgo utensils and eat it with tortilla chips! *Serves 4*

Place the ground beef in a large skillet over medium-high heat and cook, stirring, until browned, about 5 minutes. Drain well.

Add the beans, tomatoes and chiles, cooked rice, and chili powder; stir and cover. Simmer until bubbling, about 5 minutes. Add the cheese, cover, and cook until the cheese is melted, 2 to 3 minutes. Serve with the tortilla or corn chips.

1 **pound lean ground beef**

1 **14-ounce can kidney beans, undrained**

1 **10-ounce can diced tomatoes and mild green chiles (such as Ro-Tel), undrained**

1 **cup cooked white rice**

2 **tablespoons chili powder**

1 **cup shredded Cheddar cheese Tortilla chips or corn chips**

Mushroom-Jack Cheesesteak Sandwiches

by Kate Jones, ourbestbites.com

- 2 tablespoons olive oil
- 1 1-pound rib-eye steak, thinly sliced
- 1 small onion, thinly sliced
- 1 cup sliced button mushrooms
   Salt and freshly ground black pepper
- 4 high-quality sandwich buns or rolls, cut in half
- 4 slices pepper Jack cheese, cut in half

Because this recipe has so few ingredients, you want to make sure the ones you do use are top quality. Tender, flavorful, thinly cut rib-eye steak is sautéed with sweet onions and tender mushrooms, seasoned with salt and freshly ground black pepper, topped with spicy pepper Jack cheese, and served on a sandwich roll for a quick, easy, delicious meal. *Serves 4*

Heat the oil in a large skillet over medium-high heat. Add the sliced steak and stir-fry until the edges of the meat are browned and the centers are still pink, 3 to 5 minutes. Add the onion and mushrooms and cook, stirring frequently, until the steak is fully cooked and browned and the vegetables are very tender, 3 to 4 more minutes. Season to taste with salt and pepper.

Reduce the heat to medium and cook until any liquid has evaporated, 3 to 5 minutes. Remove from the heat. Divide the steak mixture among the buns or rolls and add 1 slice of cheese to each sandwich. Serve the sandwiches immediately, or heat in the broiler for about 1 minute to toast the buns and melt the cheese.

MAKE IT EASY

To get your steak sliced really thin, you can either ask the butcher to slice it for you or you can stick the steak in the freezer for 1 to 2 hours, or until it's solid but can still be pierced with the tip of a sharp knife. Then use the slicing blade on your food processor to slice the steak into thin pieces.

Dirty Rice *by Christy Jordan*, southernplate.com

This is a classic Cajun dish that brings rice to a whole new level of flavorful! It's not too spicy for children, either—my son and daughter always ask for seconds whenever I serve this handy one-dish meal. I like to double the recipe to make sure I have leftovers for lunch the following day, too. *Serves 4*

Place the ground beef, bell pepper, onion, garlic, and parsley in a large skillet over medium heat. Cook, stirring and breaking up the meat, until the beef is fully cooked and the vegetables are tender, about 15 minutes. Add the Cajun seasoning and stir. Add the cooked rice and cook, stirring, just until the rice is hot, no more than 5 minutes. Serve immediately.

1 pound lean ground beef
½ cup chopped green bell pepper
½ cup chopped onion
2 tablespoons minced garlic
¼ cup chopped fresh Italian parsley or 2 tablespoons dried parsley
2 tablespoons Cajun seasoning, or to taste
4 cups cooked rice

MAKE IT EASY
When bell peppers are in season, I like to wash and chop them to freeze for use at a later date. Simply stem, seed, and chop the bell peppers and spread them out on a baking sheet. Place the sheet in the freezer for 1 to 2 hours, then transfer the bell peppers to a large resealable plastic bag and return to the freezer, where they can be stored for up to 4 months. The same method may be used for onions as well.

"The wonderful thing about slow cooking is that with minimal effort, a home-cooked meal can be ready and waiting when you come home after a long day. The aroma that hits you when you open the door is amazing—an instant spirit-reviver."

—Rachel Rappaport

Korean Short Ribs *by Rachel Rappaport,* coconutandlime.com

½ cup soy sauce

½ cup rice wine vinegar

2 tablespoons dark brown sugar

1 teaspoon toasted sesame oil

3 pounds beef short ribs

4 garlic cloves, sliced

1 pound potatoes, peeled and cubed

2 onions, halved and sliced

2 scallions, cut into 2-inch strips

2 carrots, peeled and cut into 1-inch chunks

Beef short ribs are amazingly tender when cooked in the slow cooker; they simply fall off the bone. This dish takes its inspiration from galbi jjim, which is a popular celebratory dish in Korea. Serve it on its own or with rice. *Serves 4 to 6*

Place the soy sauce, vinegar, brown sugar, and sesame oil in a medium bowl and whisk to combine. Set the sauce aside.

Bring a large pot of water to a boil. Add the short ribs and boil until the fat is rendered, about 10 minutes. Using tongs, transfer the ribs to a slow cooker. Add the garlic, potatoes, onions, scallions, carrots, and sauce to the slow cooker. Cover and cook on low until the beef is tender, about 8 hours. Serve hot.

MAKE IT EASY

Do your prep for this recipe the night before, pop everything in the slow cooker in the morning, and dinner is served in the evening!

Stir-Fried Beef & Shiitake Mushrooms with Thai Basil *by Lori Lange*, recipegirl.com

This stir-fry combines meat and vegetables in a sauce so delicious that children will gobble it up, vegetables and all, without question. Serve it over a mound of fluffy white rice and you'll have one happy family! *Serves 4*

For Sauce: Place all the sauce ingredients in a small bowl, stir to combine, and set aside.

For Stir-Fry: Heat 1 tablespoon of the oil in a wok or large skillet over high heat. Add the onion and eggplant and stir-fry until the vegetables begin to soften, 2 to 3 minutes. Add the mushrooms and cook, stirring, until they begin to soften, 1 minute longer. Transfer the cooked vegetables to a medium bowl.

Heat the remaining 1 tablespoon oil in the same pan over high heat. Add the garlic and stir-fry until fragrant, about 30 seconds. Add the steak and stir-fry until it is lightly brown and some parts are still pink, 3 to 4 minutes. Add the chiles and sauce and simmer, stirring occasionally, until the beef is no longer pink, about 3 minutes. Remove from the heat and stir in the cooked vegetables and basil. Serve over the hot cooked rice.

FOR SAUCE:
- 4 tablespoons water
- 3 tablespoons oyster sauce
- 1½ tablespoons sweet red chili sauce

FOR STIR-FRY:
- 2 tablespoons canola oil, divided
- 1 medium onion, sliced
- ½ large Chinese eggplant, cut into ¼-inch-thick slices
- 1 cup thinly sliced shiitake mushrooms
- 4 garlic cloves, finely chopped
- 1 pound flank or skirt steak, thinly cut against the grain
- 2 Thai chiles, crushed
- 1½ cups (packed) Thai basil leaves
  Hot cooked rice

THREE

Pork

Pork Medallions with Shallots, Dried Cherries, & Spinach

by Shauna James Ahern and Daniel Ahern, **glutenfreegirl.com**

1   **cup dried cherries**

1   **cup port**

1½ **pounds boneless pork loin, sliced into eight 1-inch-thick pieces**

    Salt and freshly ground black pepper

4   **tablespoons olive oil, divided**

1½ **cups thinly sliced shallots**

1   **tablespoon finely chopped fresh rosemary**

1   **tablespoon thinly sliced garlic**

1   **pound spinach, washed and dried**

Pork is good. We love pork in this house. There are so many pork dishes that require low, slow cooking to become succulent. But sometimes you want good pork fast. In that case, try this pork medallion dish. *Serves 4*

Place the dried cherries and port in a medium bowl. Set aside, soaking the cherries in the port for 30 minutes. Season the pork to taste with salt and pepper.

Heat 1 tablespoon of the oil in a large skillet over medium-high heat. Add 2 pork medallions to the skillet and sear until golden-brown, about 3 minutes per side. Transfer the cooked pork to a plate. Repeat with the remaining oil and pork medallions.

Add the shallots to the skillet. Cook, stirring frequently, until caramelized, about 3 minutes. Add the rosemary and garlic and cook, stirring, until fragrant, about 1 minute. Drain and add the port-soaked cherries and cook for 1 minute, then add the spinach. Cook until the spinach begins to wilt, about 1 minute, then remove from the heat. Season to taste with salt and pepper. To serve, place a mound of the spinach mixture on each plate, then top each with 2 pork medallions.

Kielbasa with Sweet Onions & Fava Beans

by Marc Matsumoto, norecipes.com

1   tablespoon vegetable oil
1   large onion, sliced
2   pounds smoked kielbasa, each
     sausage scored every ½ inch
1   cup shelled and peeled fresh
     fava beans
⅓   cup beer
1   tablespoon honey mustard
     Salt and freshly ground black
     pepper
     Crusty bread or boiled potatoes

Smoked kielbasa, also known as Polish sausage, is a great sausage to keep around because it will keep forever in your freezer and can be called upon at a moment's notice to infuse pastas, soups, and stews with a boatload of flavor.

The simple meal here can be pulled together in about 10 minutes. The smoky sausage is highlighted with sweet caramelized onions and fava beans in a sauce made from beer and mustard. It's the kind of meal you'd image an Eastern European lumberjack putting down, along with a tall Pilsner, after a long day of work. *Serves 4*

Place the oven rack in the top position, put a broiler pan on the rack, and pre-heat the broiler. Heat the oil in a medium pan over medium-high heat. Add the onion and cook, stirring, until golden-brown, about 10 minutes.

While the onion is cooking, place the sausages in the preheated broiler pan, transfer to the broiler, and broil until the sausages are golden-brown, 3 to 5 minutes per side.

Add the fava beans, beer, and mustard to the pan with the onions. Season to taste with salt and pepper and bring the mixture to a boil. Boil until the beer has reduced and thickened and the fava beans are fully cooked, 3 to 4 minutes. Serve the kielbasa and onions and fava beans with crusty toasted bread or boiled potatoes.

Marc Matsumoto, norecipes.com

Marc Matsumoto is a freelance writer, photographer, and private chef who was born in Japan, grew up in Napa, and currently calls New York City home. He's loved cooking since before he could see over the kitchen counter, and while he's spent the better part of his professional life as a marketing executive, he's finally finding his niche in the world of food.

Through his website, No Recipes (norecipes.com), Marc teaches people basic techniques and introduces them to new ingredients, while giving them the confidence and inspiration to try cooking foods that may be unfamiliar. It's Marc's belief that food is one of the best ways to learn about another culture and he's recently launched Wandering Cook (wanderingcook.com) to share his adventures in food around the world.

More About Marc

What do you always have in your shopping cart?

I'm usually not one of those shoppers who shows up at the store with a list. I like buying whatever is fresh and on sale. I do like loading up on a lot of vegetables and fruits, though.

What's your go-to weeknight dinner?

Usually it's whatever is in the fridge from my biweekly shopping trip, but if I'm really in a pinch, I'll make a pasta. I always have some olive oil, a scrap of cheese, garlic, and dry pasta sitting around, and that's all you really need to make a great pasta dish.

What's your favorite kitchen tool?

I'm pretty bad about collecting kitchen gadgets, but when it comes down to it, my chef's knife and cutting board are really the only things I end up using for every meal. That said, I do love my potato ricer.

Is there anything you just can't eat?

It's a Korean delicacy called hongeohoe, skate that's been fermented at room temperature for days. The sharp ammonia smell will blast its way through even the most congested sinuses.

Blueberry Pulled Pork *by Rachel Rappaport,* coconutandlime.com

2 **pounds boneless pork roast, trimmed of excess fat**
1 **cup fresh blueberries**
1 **large onion, diced**
½ **cup chili sauce**
¼ **cup balsamic vinegar**
3 **garlic cloves, minced**
1 **teaspoon mesquite liquid smoke**
1 **teaspoon freshly ground black pepper**
1 **teaspoon smoked paprika**
½ **teaspoon cayenne pepper**
¼ **teaspoon salt**

There is no reason to use your slow cooker only during the winter months. It is perfectly suited to warm weather use, because you can make a hot meal without heating up the kitchen. Using fresh, in-season ingredients is a great way to make a slow-cooker dish taste more summery. In this dish, the blueberries nearly melt away, creating a rich sauce for the pork. *Serves 4 to 6*

Place all the ingredients in a slow cooker. Cover and cook on low until the meat shreds easily with a fork, 8 to 9 hours.

Remove the pork from the slow cooker. Shred with a fork and set aside. Using a potato masher, mash any solid bits of the sauce in the slow cooker.

Return the pork to the slow cooker and toss to coat the pork evenly with the sauce. Serve hot.

MAKE IT EASY
Do your prep ahead so you can save time in the morning. Chop the onion and garlic the night before and store them in a resealable bag in the refrigerator. Whisk together the chili sauce, vinegar, and liquid smoke in a small bowl and refrigerate. Measure out the spices and put them in the slow cooker. The next morning, all you have to do is add the sauces, pork, and blueberries to the slow cooker and turn it on before you head to work.

Greek-Style Pork Pitas *by Sara Wells, ourbestbites.com*

This quick, Greek-inspired sandwich is great for either dinner or lunch. If you don't have pork on hand, feel free to substitute thinly sliced chicken or steak for equally delicious results. *Serves 4*

Place the pork, oil, garlic, lemon juice, oregano, ½ teaspoon of the kosher salt, and the pepper in a shallow dish and toss to combine; set aside.

Place the yogurt, lemon zest, parsley, and the remaining ¼ teaspoon kosher salt in a medium bowl and stir to combine; cover and refrigerate until ready to use.

Place the tomato, cucumber, and onion in another medium bowl and toss to combine; set aside.

Heat a medium skillet over medium-high heat. Add the pork mixture to the skillet and cook, stirring frequently, until the pork is fully cooked, 3 to 4 minutes. Remove from the heat.

To assemble, place 1 lettuce leaf in each pita half. Divide the pork mixture among the pita halves, add the cucumber and tomato mixture, and top with the yogurt sauce. Serve immediately.

- ¾ pound boneless pork loin chops, cut into ¼-inch-thick slices
- 1 tablespoon olive oil
- 2 teaspoons minced garlic
- 1½ tablespoons fresh lemon juice
- 2 teaspoons minced fresh oregano
- ¾ teaspoon kosher salt, divided
- ¼ teaspoon freshly ground black pepper
- 6 tablespoons Greek yogurt
- ½ teaspoon lemon zest
- ½ tablespoon minced fresh Italian parsley
- ¼ cup diced tomato
- ¼ cup diced cucumber
- 2 tablespoons diced red onion
- 4 lettuce leaves
- 2 pita breads, each cut in half

MAKE IT EASY

To make assembly even faster, prep both the yogurt sauce and the cucumber-tomato mixture 1 day ahead and store them in the fridge until ready to use.

Make Your Own Greek-Style Yogurt: If you don't have Greek yogurt, line a fine-mesh strainer with 2 paper towels and set the strainer over a bowl. Put plain yogurt on the paper towels and let it strain in the fridge overnight to yield a much thicker yogurt.

Sweet-and-Sour Pork Stir-Fry *by Sara Wells, ourbestbites.com*

3 teaspoons vegetable oil, divided
1 pound boneless pork loin chops or pork tenderloin, cut into ¼-inch-thick slices
½ teaspoon kosher salt
¼ teaspoon freshly ground black pepper
2 garlic cloves, minced
1 tablespoon minced fresh ginger
3 cups broccoli florets
1 medium red bell pepper, stemmed, seeded, and cut into ½-inch squares
1 tablespoon cornstarch
2 tablespoons cold water
1 8-ounce can pineapple chunks, drained and juices reserved
3 tablespoons ketchup
1 tablespoon soy sauce
2 tablespoons brown sugar
1 teaspoon rice vinegar
Hot cooked white rice

Skip takeout and make something just as delicious in less than 30 minutes. In this recipe, fresh vegetables and tender pork are lightly coated in an easy sweet-and-sour sauce. *Serves 4*

Heat 2 teaspoons of the oil in a wok or large skillet over medium-high heat. Add the pork, kosher salt, black pepper, garlic, and ginger. Stir-fry until the pork is cooked and no longer pink, 3 to 4 minutes. Remove the pork from the pan and cover to keep warm.

Add the remaining 1 teaspoon oil to the pan and add the broccoli and bell pepper. Stir-fry over medium-high heat until the vegetables are crisp-tender and the broccoli is bright green, 3 to 4 minutes.

While the vegetables are cooking, place the cornstarch and cold water in a medium bowl and stir to dissolve. Add the reserved pineapple juice, ketchup, soy sauce, brown sugar, and vinegar to the bowl and stir to combine.

Return the pork mixture to the pan and add the pineapple chunks and sauce mixture. Bring to a simmer and cook until the pork and pineapple are hot and the sauce has thickened, 1 to 2 minutes. Serve the sweet and sour pork over the hot cooked rice.

MAKE IT EASY
Stock your refrigerator with bottled minced ginger, for use when a recipe calls for fresh ginger.

Pork Chop Biscuits *by Christy Jordan,* southernplate.com

This is one of those meals I like to make on evenings when family activities have us all going in different directions. Filling and delicious, it's the perfect homemade version of fast food—it can easily be wrapped in foil and taken along with us! *Serves 4*

Place the flour, salt, and pepper in a shallow dish and stir to combine. Coat chops on both sides with the flour mixture. Repeat with the remaining pork chops.

Heat the oil in a large skillet over medium heat. Add the pork chops, working in batches if necessary, and cook until browned, 4 to 5 minutes per side. Serve the pork chops on the biscuits.

1 cup all-purpose flour
1 teaspoon salt, or to taste
1 teaspoon freshly ground black pepper, or to taste
4 ½-inch thick boneless pork chops
¼ cup vegetable oil
4 biscuits

Maple-Rosemary Pork Satay
by Julie Van Rosendaal, **dinnerwithjulie.com**

Who doesn't love food on a stick? This recipe is easy to double if you want to serve a crowd—the satays are perfect for the barbecue, or they can be cooked in the oven, under the broiler. Make this a day before you want to cook and serve it; it needs that long for the flavors to meld.

The marinade works just as well with strips of chicken or turkey.

Serves 4

Cut the pork crosswise in half, then lengthwise into even strips about ½-inch thick. Place the pork strips, maple syrup, lemon juice, soy sauce, mustard, and rosemary in a large resealable plastic bag. Knead the bag gently to combine; marinate in the refrigerator for 24 hours.

Prepare the grill to medium-high. Soak bamboo skewers in water for 30 minutes, then thread the pork onto the skewers. Grill until just cooked through, about 2 minutes per side. Serve hot or cold.

1   1- to 1½-pound pork tenderloin
¼   cup maple syrup
3   tablespoons fresh or bottled
    lemon juice
3   tablespoons soy sauce
2   tablespoons Dijon mustard
2   tablespoons chopped fresh
    rosemary

MAKE IT EASY
Make this ahead and freeze before grilling; the uncooked pork and marinade will keep in an airtight container for up to 6 months.

Pork

Bourbon Pork Tenderloin *by Catherine McCord,* **weelicious.com**

- ¼ cup bourbon
- ¼ cup Dijon mustard
- ¼ cup soy sauce
- 1 tablespoon grated fresh ginger
- 1 garlic clove, chopped
- 2 tablespoons vegetable or canola oil
- 2 pork tenderloins (about 1¼ pounds each), silver skin removed

This dish has been one of the tried-and-true recipes in my family since I was a little girl. Even today, when friends and family come over for dinner, it's the most requested dish I make—lucky for me it's so easy. It looks really elegant and tastes unbelievably delicious, but it only takes minutes to prepare. Serve the pork with mashed potatoes and roasted vegetables. *Serves 4*

Place the bourbon, mustard, soy sauce, ginger, garlic, and oil in a large resealable plastic bag; seal the bag and shake to combine. Add the pork, kneading to coat. Marinate in the refrigerator for 4 to 24 hours.

Prepare the grill to high. Remove the pork from the marinade, discard the marinade, and grill the tenderloins until they are golden-brown and the internal temperature is 140°F, 7 to 9 minutes per side.

Remove the pork from the grill and let it rest for 5 to 10 minutes before slicing.

MAKE IT EASY

Want to serve this with a sauce? Double your marinade, set aside half of it, and boil the reserved half until it thickens, about 5 minutes.

Kielbasa & Cabbage Skillet
by Christy Jordan, **southernplate.com**

I've always loved skillet meals because they are so fuss-free and easy to pull together. Having only one skillet to clean when I'm done is always a plus, too! Granny made all of her skillet meals in cast iron, but you can use whatever type of skillet you prefer; it will still taste just as good as hers did.

I like to serve this recipe with cornbread. You can also serve it as a side dish. *Serves 4*

¼ **cup vegetable oil or olive oil**
½ **pound kielbasa, sliced**
1 **small cabbage, chopped**
5 **tablespoons water**
1 **tablespoon salt**

Heat the oil in a large skillet over medium heat. Add the sliced kielbasa and cook, stirring, until browned, about 5 minutes. Add the cabbage, water, and salt. Cover, increase the heat to high, and cook, stirring, until the cabbage is tender, about 5 minutes. Serve immediately.

Five-Spice Pork Chops with Hoisin Glaze

by Marc Matsumoto, **norecipes.com**

Found in Asian markets or the Asian foods section of the supermarket, Chinese five-spice powder is a potent blend of star anise, cinnamon, Sichuan peppercorns, cloves, and fennel seeds. I love pairing it with meats such as pork because of its sweet complexity.

This recipe uses thin-cut pork chops, which cook quickly and have more surface area to which the sweet hoisin sauce can adhere. You can serve these with either rice or potatoes, and if you somehow manage to end up with leftovers, they're perfect in a sandwich for lunch the next day. *Serves 4*

Rub the pork chops with the garlic and season with the Chinese five-spice powder and salt.

Heat the oil in a large skillet over medium-high heat. Working in batches, add the pork in a single layer and cook until browned and fully cooked, about 2 minutes per side. Transfer the cooked pork chops to a plate.

To make the glaze, drain the pan of any excess oil, then add the hoisin sauce, rice wine or sherry, and honey, and stir to combine. Bring the sauce to a boil, scraping the browned bits from the bottom of the pan. Continue boiling until the sauce forms a thick, glossy glaze, 1 to 2 minutes. Return the pork chops to the pan and toss to coat evenly with the sauce. To serve, top the pork chops with the scallion and serve with the hot cooked rice and steamed bok choy.

1 **pound pork chops, ¼ inch thick**
2 **garlic cloves, minced**
2 **teaspoons Chinese five-spice powder**
  Salt
2 **tablespoons vegetable oil**
¼ **cup hoisin sauce**
2 **tablespoons Shaohxing rice wine or dry sherry**
2 **tablespoons honey**
1 **scallion (green part), thinly sliced on the diagonal**
  Hot cooked white rice
  Steamed bok choy

Pork

121

"We both feel that it's important to really cook on weeknights and not just rush through it. Being in the kitchen together, preparing that meal, is one of the best times of the day."

–Shauna James Ahern and Daniel Ahern

Pork Cutlets with Apple-Bacon Sauce

by Lori Lange, recipegirl.com

1 cup uncooked rice

4 slices pork tenderloin (about 1 pound), pounded to a ½-inch thickness between 2 sheets of plastic wrap

¼ teaspoon salt

¼ teaspoon freshly ground black pepper

2 slices bacon, finely chopped

¼ cup minced onion

1¼ cups unsweetened apple juice

½ cup chopped Granny Smith apple, unpeeled

Pork tenderloin's moist and tender nature makes me favor it over the ubiquitous pork chop. Chunks of tenderloin are easy to lightly pound into cutlets, and they cook up quickly in a pan. A simple apple-bacon sauce tops off these cutlets. *Serves 4*

Cook the rice according to the package instructions. Season the pork with the salt and pepper.

While the rice is cooking, place the bacon in a large skillet over medium heat and cook until crisp, about 5 minutes. Remove the bacon from the skillet, reserving the fat in the skillet, and set aside.

Increase the heat to medium-high. Add the pork to the skillet, cover, and cook until fully cooked and no longer pink, about 3 minutes per side. Transfer the pork to a plate and cover to keep warm.

Add the onion to the skillet and cook over medium-high heat, stirring, until softened, about 2 minutes. Add the apple juice and bring to a boil. Cook until the liquid is reduced to about ½ cup, about 4 minutes. Add the cooked bacon and apple and cook for 1 minute. Remove from the heat. Serve the pork cutlets over the prepared rice, topping the cutlets with the apple-bacon sauce.

Pork, Asparagus, & Ginger Pot Stickers

by Julie Van Rosendaal, dinnerwithjulie.com

If you want your pot stickers leaner than the ones in this recipe, but just as flavorful, buy a pork tenderloin, cut it into chunks, and pulse it in the food processor (or run it through a food mill) until ground—tenderloin is leaner than most packaged ground pork.

These dumplings can be made ahead, wrapped, and frozen for up to four months, for use in wonton soup—instead of cooking them in the skillet, toss them into simmering broth and cook until they float to the surface. Add a handful of bok choy and serve over a shallow bowl of noodles. *Serves 6*

Add the ground pork, asparagus, scallions, soy sauce, garlic, ginger, sesame oil, sugar, and chili sauce, if desired, to a medium bowl and combine, using your hands.

To fill the wontons, place a small spoonful of filling in the middle of each wrapper; use your finger to moisten the edges of the wrapper with water, then fold the wrapper over, pressing the edge tightly to seal as you press out any air bubbles. Place the dumplings, seam side up, on a baking sheet, pressing lightly to flatten the bottoms. Cover the dumplings with a dish towel or plastic wrap to prevent them from drying out. (The dumplings can be prepared up to this point, covered with plastic wrap, and refrigerated for up to 24 hours or frozen.)

When ready to cook the pot stickers, heat the canola oil in a large heavy skillet over medium-high heat. Working in batches, place about half of the dumplings in the skillet and cook until the bottoms are golden-brown, 1 to 2 minutes.

Add ¼ cup broth or water to the pan. Cover, reduce the heat to medium, and cook until the pot stickers are fully steamed, about 5 minutes. Repeat with the remaining pot stickers, adding additional broth or water. Serve the pot stickers with the hot cooked rice and with soy sauce or plum sauce on the side.

1 pound lean ground pork
5 asparagus stalks, trimmed and finely chopped
2 scallions, finely chopped
1 tablespoon soy sauce
1 garlic clove, crushed
2 teaspoons grated fresh ginger
1 teaspoon toasted sesame oil
½ teaspoon sugar
⅛ teaspoon hot chili sauce (optional)
1 12-ounce package wonton wrappers, thawed if frozen
1 tablespoon canola oil
½ to ¾ cup chicken broth, vegetable broth, or water, divided
Hot cooked rice
Soy sauce or bottled plum sauce

Cemita de Carnitas *by Matt Armendariz,* **mattbites.com**

1 pound cooked carnitas

1 sliced avocado or 1 cup
   guacamole

½ pound Oaxacan string cheese or
   panela cheese

½ small onion, sliced

1 jalapeño chile, seeded and
   sliced into rings

4 seeded egg rolls, brioche buns,
   or sandwich rolls, split

This Mexican sandwich is messy, delicious, and guaranteed to hit the spot. Traditionally, it calls for a seeded egg roll, but you can easily substitute brioche for an equally tasty result. Find the Oaxacan string cheese or panela cheese, both soft white cheeses, in Latin markets. Pre-seasoned carnitas can be found in Latin markets and also at specialty grocery stores. *Serves 4*

Divide the carnitas, avocado or guacamole, cheese, onion, and jalapeño among the 4 rolls or buns. Serve immediately.

Pork Chops & Plum Sauce

by Shauna James Ahern and Daniel Ahern, glutenfreegirl.com

The sweet tartness of Italian plums is softened by warm butter and enhanced by puckery orange juice—this sauce lingers in the mind long after it is gone. If Italian prune plums can't be found, you can use another variety. Be sure you don't skip the inverted saucer when you let the pork chops rest; the saucer keeps them from sitting in their own juices. Serve the pork chops with a side of steamed green beans. *Serves 4*

Preheat the oven to 450°F. Season both sides of the pork chops with salt and pepper. Heat the oil in a large sauté pan over medium-high heat. Add 2 pork chops and cook until golden-brown, about 4 minutes per side, then transfer the seared chops to a large baking dish; repeat with the remaining chops, and set the sauté pan aside.

Place the seared chops in the oven and bake until the meat closest to the bone is only slightly pink and the internal temperature reaches 150°F, 12 to 15 minutes. Remove the pork chops from the oven and let them rest for 5 minutes on an inverted saucer on a large plate. Set the baking dish aside, reserving the cooking juices in the dish.

While the pork chops are in the oven, place 3 tablespoons of the butter in the large sauté pan and melt over medium-high heat until bubbly, being careful not to brown it, about 1 minute. Add the onion and cook, stirring, until softened, about 5 minutes. Add the plums and cook until they begin to soften, 3 to 4 minutes. Add the sugar and balsamic vinegar and simmer until the plums are fully softened, about 5 more minutes. Add the orange juice and cook until the liquid is reduced by two-thirds, 5 to 6 minutes.

Strain the sauce and transfer it to the baking dish with the reserved cooking juices. Cook the sauce over high heat until it has reduced and thickened, 5 to 6 minutes. Add the remaining 1 tablespoon butter and stir until blended and emulsified. Spoon the plum sauce over the pork chops and serve with the steamed green beans.

4   center-cut pork chops, fat still
      on, 2 inches thick
      Salt and freshly ground pepper
2   tablespoons canola oil
4   tablespoons (½ stick) unsalted
      butter, divided
1   medium red onion, finely diced
12 Italian prune plums, quartered
      and pitted
¼   cup sugar
3   tablespoons white balsamic
      vinegar
½   cup orange juice
      Steamed green beans

Panini with Prosciutto, Fontina, Spinach, & Slow-Roasted Tomatoes

by Andrea Meyers, andreasrecipes.com

8 slices whole grain bread

8 slices prosciutto or other thinly
    sliced ham

¼ pound fontina or Swiss cheese,
    grated

1 cup sautéed spinach or 1 cup
    (packed) raw baby spinach

8 sun-dried tomatoes
    Extra-virgin olive oil

Panini and other grilled sandwiches are great for busy weeknight meals. Try gathering an assortment of meats, cheeses, and other fillings, then let everyone choose his or her own favorite combination. Just add a side salad and you have a fast, light meal. *Serves 4*

Heat a panini press or panini pan, or prepare the grill to medium heat. Place 1 slice of bread on a plate. Add 2 slices of prosciutto, one-fourth of the cheese, ¼ cup spinach, and 2 tomato halves or sun-dried tomatoes, topping with another slice of bread. Repeat with the remaining ingredients. Brush one side of each sandwich with oil.

Place a sandwich on the panini press or grill pan, oiled side down, and brush more oil on the top. Close the panini press and grill until the cheese sizzles, 2 to 3 minutes; if using a grill pan, grill the sandwich for 2 to 3 minutes on each side. Remove from the heat and let the sandwich cool for 1 minute before slicing on the diagonal. Repeat with the remaining sandwiches and serve immediately.

Chop Suey *by Marc Matsumoto,* norecipes.com

Chop suey is a stir-fried dish that includes a variety of meat and vegetables in a thick, savory sauce. While there are theories that it originated in the Guangdong province of China, chop suey is now widely believed to have originated in the United States during construction of the transcontinental railway.

In this version, I've given chop suey a makeover, loading it up with vegetables and cutting back on the grease. Served over noodles or rice, it makes for a quick, balanced weeknight meal that's sure to please. *Serves 4*

Place the pork, rice wine or sherry, oyster sauce, 1 teaspoon of the cornstarch, and white pepper to taste in a large bowl and toss gently to combine; marinate in the refrigerator for at least 1 hour and up to 2 days.

Place the chicken broth and remaining 5 teaspoons cornstarch in a medium bowl and stir to combine. Set aside.

Prepare the chow mein noodles according to the package instructions. Drain and add the sesame oil, tossing gently to prevent the noodles from sticking together. Set aside.

Heat the vegetable oil in a wok or large skillet over high heat. Add the garlic and swirl the pan to distribute. Add the pork and stir-fry until no longer pink, about 2 minutes. Transfer the pork to a plate and set aside.

Add the celery, onion, carrot, mushrooms, and cabbage to the pan and cook until they are brightly colored, 1 to 2 minutes. Add the sugar snap peas and cooked pork, then add the chicken broth mixture and bring to a boil. Once boiling, cook until the sauce has thickened, about 1 minute. Serve the chop suey over the prepared chow mein noodles.

½   **pound pork loin, cut into ¼-inch-wide strips**
1   **tablespoon Shaohxing rice wine or dry sherry**
1   **tablespoon oyster sauce**
6   **teaspoons cornstarch, divided**
    Freshly ground white pepper
2   **cups chicken broth**
1   **6-ounce package chow mein noodles**
2   **tablespoons toasted sesame oil**
1   **tablespoon vegetable oil**
3   **garlic cloves, minced**
1   **celery stalk, diced**
½   **medium onion, diced**
1   **small carrot, shredded**
8   **button mushrooms, quartered**
3   **green cabbage leaves, chopped**
15   **sugar snap peas, trimmed**

Smoked Sausage Sandwiches with Peppers & Onions
by Sara Wells, ourbestbites.com

¾ pound cooked smoked pork sausage, cut into ¼-inch-thick pieces

3 tablespoons plus 1 teaspoon olive oil, divided

1 large red bell pepper, stemmed, seeded, and thinly sliced

1 small onion, thinly sliced

¼ teaspoon kosher salt

⅛ teaspoon freshly ground black pepper

4 6-inch hoagie rolls

4 slices provolone cheese

Because the smoked sausage in this recipe is already cooked, heating it up is done in a flash. Featuring sautéed peppers and onions, melted cheese, and a toasted bun, this sandwich is both quick and satisfying. For a lighter version, try smoked turkey sausage instead of pork sausage. *Serves 4*

Preheat the broiler. Place the sausage pieces in a medium skillet over medium-high heat. Cook, stirring, until golden-brown, 2 to 3 minutes. Remove the sausage pieces from the skillet and cover to keep them warm.

Add 1 teaspoon of the oil, the bell pepper, onion, kosher salt, and black pepper to the skillet. Cook over medium-high heat, stirring, until the vegetables are tender, 5 to 7 minutes.

While the pepper and onion are cooking, slice open the rolls and brush the insides lightly with the remaining 3 tablespoons oil. Broil the rolls until golden-brown, about 30 seconds. (Keep the broiler on.)

When the vegetables are tender, return the sausage pieces to the skillet and cook until the sausage pieces are hot, about 1 minute. Divide the sausage mixture among the 4 rolls and add 1 slice of cheese to each sandwich. Broil the sandwiches for just a few seconds, until the cheese is melted. Serve immediately.

Sara Wells, ourbestbites.com

Sara Wells was born and raised near Seattle, Washington. The lush green surroundings inspired her to study horticulture at Brigham Young University and earn a degree in landscape design. While she's always loved cooking, during her college years she spent a year and a half living in southern Brazil, where she developed a special love for Latin-inspired cuisine. She combines her talent for art and design with her love of food to create dishes that not only taste great but are visually appealing and fun to eat as well.

Sara co-authors the hit food blog Our Best Bites (ourbestbites.com) with her good friend Kate Jones. As mothers of young children, the two women create family-friendly meals and share tips to make life in the kitchen easier and more enjoyable. Sara currently resides in Boise, Idaho, with her husband and three young sons.

More About Sara

What do you always have in your shopping cart?
Garlic, limes, chocolate, and at least one toddler begging for cookies.

What's your go-to weeknight dinner?
Grilled chicken and black beans over rice, with lots of fresh lime juice on top. It's comfort food from my time spent in Brazil that my whole family loves.

What's your favorite kitchen tool?
My garlic press. I literally use it every day!

Is there anything you just can't eat?
Seafood. Which, sadly, is a complete embarrassment because of my Seattle heritage.

Pulled Pork Pizza *by Julie Van Rosendaal,* dinnerwithjulie.com

FOR PULLED PORK:

- 1 1½-pound pork tenderloin or 1 to 2 pounds pork shoulder
  Salt and freshly ground black pepper
- 2 tablespoons canola or olive oil
- 1 12-ounce bottle dark beer, apple cider, or apple juice, divided
- ¼ cup barbecue sauce, or to taste

FOR PIZZA:

- 1 pound pizza dough or 1 prepared pizza crust
- 1 cup shredded mozzarella cheese, or to taste
  Chopped fresh cilantro leaves, for garnish (optional)

A pulled pork pizza is a wonderful thing. Make the pulled pork in advance; it requires only a few minutes of prep time before spending a few hours in the slow cooker. If you're making this for the kids, you can use apple juice or cider instead of beer. *Serves 4*

For Pulled Pork: Season all sides of the pork to taste with salt and pepper. Heat the oil in a large skillet over medium-high heat; add the pork and cook until browned, about 3 minutes per side. Transfer the pork to a slow cooker. Pour about half of the beer, cider, or juice into the skillet and swirl gently; use a spatula to loosen the browned pork pieces in the skillet. Transfer the skillet mixture to the slow cooker and add the remaining beer, cider, or juice. Cover and cook on low for 6 hours.

When the pork is cooked, drain and reserve the liquid, and shred the meat with a fork. Add the barbecue sauce and, if the pork seems dry, several tablespoons of the reserved liquid. Toss until the meat is moistened but not too saucy. (The pork can be prepared up to this point and refrigerated in an airtight container for 3 days or frozen for up to 3 months. Reheat over low heat on the stovetop, with a spoonful of water to help get it going.)

For Pizza: Preheat the oven to 450°F. If using pizza dough, roll or pat the dough into a rough circle or oval on a flour- or cornmeal-dusted baking sheet. Bake until set and barely golden, about 10 minutes.

Spread the pulled pork mixture over the pizza crust and top with the cheese. Bake until the crust is golden and the cheese is melted, 10 to 15 minutes. Remove from the oven and garnish with cilantro, if desired. Serve immediately.

MAKE IT EASY

Browning the pork first adds flavor, but you can skip that step and just toss everything in the slow cooker. If you like, make a bigger batch of pulled pork (increase the quantity of pork and barbecue sauce, but stick to 1 bottle of beer, cider, or juice) and freeze the extra pork for another quick pizza later on. The pork freezes well in an airtight container for up to 3 months.

FOUR

Seafood

Seared Fish with Green-Mango Pico de Gallo
by Marc Matsumoto, norecipes.com

1 firm green (underripe) mango, peeled and cut into ⅛-inch cubes

¼ cup finely diced red bell pepper

¼ cup finely diced red onion

1 tablespoon finely chopped fresh cilantro leaves

1 tablespoon fresh lime juice

½ teaspoon kosher salt, plus additional for seasoning

1 serrano chile, seeded and finely chopped (optional)

1 teaspoon hot sauce (optional)

1 tablespoon oil

4 skin-on salmon fillets (about 1½ pounds)

Freshly ground black pepper

Inspired by the tropics, this green-mango pico de gallo creates a wonderful contrast of flavor, color, and texture for fish. In place of salmon, you can also use swordfish or halibut. *Serves 4*

Place the mango, bell pepper, onion, cilantro, lime juice, kosher salt, chile, and hot sauce in a medium bowl and toss to combine; set the pico de gallo aside. Heat the oil in a large skillet over medium heat. Pat the salmon fillets dry and season to taste with salt and black pepper. Place the fillets in the pan, skin side down, and cook until the skin is browned and crisp. Turn over the fillets with a spatula and cook until the fish is browned and the meat flakes easily. To serve, top each cooked fillet with the green-mango pico de gallo.

Salmon Wellington Puff Pastry Squares with Creamy Parmesan Sauce *by Lori Lange, recipegirl.com*

1 tablespoon butter

½ pound sliced button mushrooms

1 large shallot, sliced

1 tablespoon finely minced fresh Italian parsley

⅛ teaspoon salt, plus additional for seasoning

⅛ teaspoon freshly ground black pepper, plus additional for seasoning

Nonstick cooking spray

1 sheet frozen puff pastry, thawed and cut into 4 squares

4 4-ounce skinless salmon fillets

2 tablespoons olive oil

⅓ cup heavy whipping cream

1 tablespoon freshly grated Parmesan cheese

1 teaspoon Dijon mustard

It may sound fancy, but this recipe is very simple. Salmon is baked on a bed of sautéed mushrooms over golden puff pastry and lightly drizzled with a creamy cheese sauce. It's a restaurant quality meal that you can get on the table in under 30 minutes. *Serves 4*

Preheat the oven to 425°F. Melt the butter in a medium skillet over medium heat. Add the mushrooms and shallot and cook, stirring, until the vegetables are softened and the liquid has evaporated, about 5 minutes. Add the parsley, salt, and pepper and stir. Transfer the mixture to a fine-mesh sieve over a bowl to drain and let it cool for about 3 minutes while preparing the puff pastry.

Line a rimmed baking sheet with foil and spray the foil with nonstick cooking spray. Place the puff pastry squares on the prepared baking sheet. Add some of the mushroom mixture to the center of each puff pastry, leaving a ½-inch border around the edge of each pastry. Top each with 1 salmon fillet. Brush the top of each salmon fillet with oil and season with salt and pepper.

Bake until the puff pastry is golden and the salmon is fully cooked and flakes easily with a fork, about 20 minutes. Remove from the oven.

Place the cream in a microwave-safe small bowl and heat in the microwave for 40 to 50 seconds, just until bubbling and hot. Add the cheese and mustard and whisk until the cheese is melted and the sauce is smooth. Serve the salmon and sauce immediately.

Pan-Seared Halibut with Picholine Olive & Sun-Dried Tomato Relish

by Daniel Ahern and Shauna James Ahern, **glutenfreegirl.com**

This dish is best made in spring and summer months, when wild-caught halibut is at its peak in taste. Look for French picholine olives, which are marinated in herbes de Provence and coriander, instead of the American-made picholines, which are brined in citric acid. Your taste buds will thank you. We recommend the sun-dried tomatoes packed in oil because they are already hydrated and ready to go. *Serves 4*

Place the olives, sun-dried tomatoes, olive oil, lemon juice, garlic, basil, and anchovy in a food processor and pulse until thoroughly chopped and combined. Season to taste with salt and pepper, if necessary. Set the picholine relish aside.

Preheat the oven to 450°F. Pat the halibut fillets dry.

Heat the canola oil in a large skillet over medium-high heat until very hot. Add 2 halibut fillets to the pan and sear until golden-brown, about 3 minutes per side. Transfer the seared fillets to a large greased baking dish. Repeat with the remaining uncooked fillets.

Transfer the seared fish to the oven and cook until the sides of the fish feel firm to the touch and the internal temperature is 120°F, about 4 minutes. Serve the fillets immediately, with the picholine relish.

- 2 cups pitted French picholine olives or other small green olives
- ½ cup chopped sun-dried tomatoes
- ¼ cup extra-virgin olive oil
- 2 tablespoons fresh lemon juice
- 1 tablespoon chopped garlic
- 6 large fresh basil leaves
- 1 anchovy fillet
  Salt and freshly ground black pepper
- 4 6-ounce wild Alaskan halibut fillets, at least 2 inches thick
- 2 tablespoons canola oil

Shrimp & Vegetable Stir-Fry
by Catherine McCord, weelicious.com

1 tablespoon vegetable or canola
  oil
1 cup snow peas
1 red bell pepper, stemmed,
  seeded, and thinly sliced
1 pound shrimp, peeled and
  deveined
½ cup chopped scallions
⅓ cup teriyaki sauce
  Hot cooked brown rice

When I was a kid, my parents would pick up Chinese takeout as a special treat. I loved every last bite, most likely because the recipes were heavy and laden with MSG. Now, as an adult, I see how easy it is to make homemade versions of some of my favorite takeout recipes, like this shrimp and vegetable stir-fry with a side of brown rice. It still has all of the flavors and textures I love, without the additives that I know aren't good for my family. Now when I want to serve a special treat, I pop this recipe into Chinese takeout containers and still have tons of fun enjoying this treat! *Serves 4*

Heat the oil in a wok or large skillet over high heat. Add the snow peas and bell pepper and stir-fry for 2 minutes. Add the shrimp and scallions and stir-fry for 2 more minutes. Add the teriyaki sauce and stir-fry until the shrimp is fully cooked and pink, about 5 more minutes. Serve immediately with the hot cooked rice.

Seared Ahi Tuna with Quinoa Salad

by Laura Levy, **laurasbestrecipes.com**

Quinoa is a wonderful source of protein and a great substitution for rice or other starchy side dishes. This recipe is great for people who want something light with low carbs. To spice up this dish, consider adding a marinade or spice rub of your choice to the tuna. You can also try this recipe with salmon. I like to use just the white parts and a little bit of the green parts of the scallions. *Serves 4*

Prepare the quinoa according to the package instructions.

Place ¼ cup of the oil, the lemon juice, garlic, chile, and honey in a medium bowl and whisk to combine. Set the lemon dressing aside.

Season the tuna steaks with salt and pepper.

Heat the remaining ¼ cup oil in a large skillet over high heat. Add the tuna steaks, leaving plenty of room between each, and cook undisturbed until they are just seared and still rare in the center, about 2 minutes per side. Remove from the heat.

Place the cooked quinoa in a large bowl. Add the scallions, cilantro, and lemon dressing and stir to combine. Serve immediately with the tuna steaks.

1 cup quinoa
½ cup olive oil, divided
¼ cup Meyer lemon juice or regular fresh lemon juice
3 garlic cloves, minced
1 Thai chile, seeded and diced
1 tablespoon honey
4 5-ounce ahi tuna steaks, 1 inch thick
Salt and freshly ground black pepper
3 scallions, thinly sliced
¼ cup chopped fresh cilantro leaves

Rosemary-Coconut Catfish *by Kath Younger,* katheats.com

1 cup regular (old-fashioned) rolled oats

½ cup ground flax seeds

½ cup unsweetened shredded coconut

2½ teaspoons chopped fresh rosemary

2 teaspoons salt

½ teaspoon freshly ground black pepper

4 6-ounce catfish fillets, ½ inch thick

2 large egg whites

Nonstick cooking spray

Fried catfish meets delicate herbs and bold coconut in this quick, easy, and healthy version of baked fish. Flax seeds and oats add nutrition and crunch, and rosemary and coconut make the catfish shine. This recipe is very versatile—sub out the rosemary and coconut for any of your favorite herbs and spices. Serve the fish with a simple salad or sautéed greens. *Serves 4*

Preheat the oven to 375°F. Place the oats, flax seeds, coconut, rosemary, salt, and pepper in a food processor and pulse until the mixture is combined but still has a crumblike consistency, about 30 seconds. Transfer the oat mixture to a large resealable plastic bag.

Pat the catfish fillets dry. Place the egg whites in a shallow bowl.

Dip each catfish fillet in the egg whites, turning to coat, and then place the fillets in the bag with the oat mixture. Shake to coat the fillets. Remove the fillets from the bag, dip each in the egg whites again, then return them to the bag to coat with the oat mixture again.

Spray a baking sheet with nonstick cooking spray and add the fish fillets. Bake until the crust is crisp and the fish flakes easily with a fork, about 25 minutes. Serve immediately.

Fish Cakes & Tartar Sauce
by Julie Van Rosendaal, dinnerwithjulie.com

Fish cakes are best made with roughly equal parts mashed potato and fish; if you remember that, the rest is pretty much up to you. Crab works just as well, and if you don't have leftover mashed potatoes, peel one or two and boil them or cook them in the microwave, then mash with a fork. (Don't worry about getting all the lumps out.) The quantities of the additions are up to you, or they are just as delicious plain. Round out this meal with a hearty green salad or some roasted vegetables.

Serves 4

Place the cooked fish, mashed potatoes, scallions, bell pepper, and herbs in a large bowl and roughly mash to combine. Form the mixture into ¾-inch-thick patties.

Place the flour, egg, and panko or breadcrumbs in 3 separate shallow bowls. Beat the egg with a fork.

Heat the oil and butter in a large skillet over medium-high heat. Dredge the patties in the flour, then the egg, and then the crumbs to coat both sides of each patty well. When the butter is melted, add the patties to the skillet, working in batches, and cook until golden-brown and crisp, about 5 minutes per side.

To make the tartar sauce, place the mayonnaise, relish, onion, mustard, and lemon juice in a small bowl and stir to combine; refrigerate until ready to serve or cover and refrigerate for up to 1 week. Serve the fish cakes warm or at room temperature with the tartar sauce.

1 cup flaked cooked cod, halibut, salmon, or tuna
1 cup mashed potatoes
¼ cup thinly sliced scallions
⅓ cup finely chopped red bell pepper
⅓ cup chopped fresh herbs (such as Italian parsley, chives, thyme, or basil)
½ cup all-purpose flour
1 large egg
1 cup panko (Japanese breadcrumbs) or other breadcrumbs
1 tablespoon canola or olive oil
1 tablespoon butter
½ cup mayonnaise (regular or light)
3 tablespoons relish or finely chopped sweet pickles
2 tablespoons finely chopped or grated onion
2 teaspoons Dijon mustard
2 teaspoons fresh or bottled lemon juice

Grilled Mahi Mahi with Grapefruit Salad & Curry Vinaigrette
by Andrea Meyers, andreasrecipes.com

Grilled mahi mahi makes a great weeknight meal because it cooks so quickly. When grilling fish make sure you brush the grill rack and rub the fish with oil to keep it from sticking, then after placing the fish on the hot grill, don't move it again until you are ready to turn it over. The curry vinaigrette will keep for a few days and you can make it ahead for even faster dinner preparation. *Serves 4*

Place 2 tablespoons of the curry powder and the water in a small bowl and stir to make a paste. Add the vinegar and sea salt and stir, then add ½ cup of the olive oil and stir. Set the curry vinaigrette aside.

In a medium bowl, rub the mahi mahi fillets with 2 tablespoons of the olive oil, then with the 2 remaining tablespoons curry powder. Set aside.

Cut off the peel and white pith from the grapefruits. Using a small sharp knife, cut between the membranes to release the grapefruit segments into a small bowl.

Brush the grill rack with canola oil and prepare the grill to medium-high. Grill the mahi mahi fillets until the fish begins to firm, about 4 minutes. Carefully turn over the fillets with a large metal spatula and grill until the fish is flaky and fully cooked, about 4 more minutes. Transfer to a platter.

Place the lettuce, cucumber, avocado, and grapefruit segments in a large bowl and toss. Drizzle the salad with the curry vinaigrette and serve with the cooked mahi mahi fillets.

- 4 **tablespoons curry powder, divided**
- 1 **tablespoon water**
- 2 **tablespoons white wine vinegar**
- ¼ **teaspoon sea salt**
- ½ **cup plus 2 tablespoons olive oil, divided**
- 4 **mahi mahi fillets**
- 2 **large ruby red grapefruits**
  Canola oil, for brushing grill
- 1 **small head Boston lettuce, torn**
- 1 **cucumber, chopped**
- 1 **avocado, peeled, pitted, and cubed**

Scallops with Parmesan-Asparagus Orzo & Bacon

by Laura Levy, laurasbestrecipes.com

1 pound medium sea scallops, trimmed

Salt and freshly ground black pepper

2 tablespoons unsalted butter

1 cup orzo

2¾ cups chicken broth

1 pound asparagus, trimmed and cut into ½-inch pieces

¼ cup freshly grated Parmesan cheese

4 slices applewood-smoked bacon, chopped

3 tablespoons extra-virgin olive oil

Thinly sliced Parmesan cheese, for garnish

This dish is also delicious with pancetta or prosciutto in place of the bacon. Look for fresh sea scallops. I enjoy the large scallops from Alaska as they are wild caught. Have fun with the orzo and add your favorite seasonal vegetables if you can't find asparagus. *Serves 4*

Place the oven rack in the top position and preheat the oven to 475°F. Pat the scallops dry and season to taste with salt and pepper. Set aside.

Melt the butter in a large skillet over high heat. Add the orzo and cook, stirring, for 1 to 2 minutes. Add the chicken broth and bring it to a boil. Reduce the heat to low, cover, and simmer, stirring occasionally, until the orzo begins to soften, 8 to 10 minutes. Add the asparagus, cover, and simmer for 5 more minutes. Uncover and cook until all the liquid is absorbed, 2 to 3 minutes. Remove the orzo from the heat and add the grated cheese. Stir and season to taste with salt and pepper.

Place the chopped bacon in an ovenproof skillet over medium-high heat. Cook until the bacon is crisp, 5 to 7 minutes per side. Transfer the bacon to a paper towel to drain. Drain the pan of all but 1 tablespoon bacon fat. Add the oil to the pan and heat over medium-high heat until the oil shimmers. Add the scallops to the pan in a single layer and sear, undisturbed, until the edges brown and the scallops begin to sizzle, about 3 minutes per side. Transfer the skillet to the top rack in the oven and bake until the scallops are golden-brown and firm, 5 to 6 minutes. Top the Parmesan-asparagus orzo with the cooked bacon and thin slices of Parmesan cheese and serve immediately with the scallops.

Baked Salmon with Seville Orange Marmalade & Wasabi

by Shauna James Ahern and Daniel Ahern, **glutenfreegirl.com**

This easy yet elegant dish will take you through an array of senses: the richness of the oils in the salmon, the spicy bite of ginger and wasabi, and the sweet bitterness of Seville orange marmalade. Make this dinner during the spring and summer, when Alaskan salmon is at the peak of its season. The fatty oils of fresh wild salmon will give you a richer flavor than you would find in any farmed salmon.

The time it will take to bake this salmon a juicy medium-rare will depend on the thickness of the piece of fish you buy. Salmon cut close to the tail will be thinner and thus take less time to cook than the fillet cut closer to the head. Use your meat thermometer as your guide. If you can't find Seville orange marmalade, regular marmalade will do. *Serves 4*

1 tablespoon canola oil
1 cup Seville orange marmalade
1 tablespoon Dijon mustard
2 teaspoons dry wasabi powder
1 teaspoon minced garlic
1 teaspoon grated fresh ginger
1 teaspoon kosher salt, divided
1 teaspoon freshly ground black pepper, divided
4 6-ounce skin-on wild salmon fillets

Preheat the oven to 425°F. Line a baking sheet with foil and brush the foil with the oil. Place the marmalade, mustard, wasabi powder, garlic, ginger, ½ teaspoon of the kosher salt, and ½ teaspoon of the pepper in a medium bowl and stir well to combine. Season the salmon fillets with the remaining kosher salt and pepper, then brush the top of each salmon fillet with about one-fourth of the marmalade mixture. Place the fillets on the baking sheet, skin side down.

Bake until the salmon flakes easily with a fork and reaches an internal temperature of 120°F, 7 to 12 minutes. Serve immediately.

Lori Lange, recipegirl.com

Lori Lange (aka "RecipeGirl") left the elementary school classroom in 2005 to start Recipe Girl (recipegirl.com), which houses more than 2,500 original and adapted recipes and entertaining menus. Lori now spends her days developing recipes and photographing food for various companies, websites, and publications as well as Recipe Girl. She has contributed to several cookbooks.

More About Lori

What do you always have in your shopping cart?

Wine, red leaf lettuce, avocados, tomatoes, Greek yogurt, eggs, butter, and my indulgences: Lucky Charms, red licorice, and root beer.

What's your go-to weeknight dinner?

Our family's favorite main-dish salad, which is composed of lettuce, tomato, avocado, mozzarella cheese, toasted pine nuts, and roasted chicken tossed with a simple dressing of white wine vinegar, Dijon mustard, olive oil, salt, and pepper. Served with a hunk of good bread, this salad makes everyone happy!

What's your favorite kitchen tool?

My zester! Seems like I'm zesting lemons and limes, Parmesan, or nutmeg pretty much every day in one recipe or another.

Is there anything you just can't eat?

Anything with tentacles, like calamari or octopus, creeps me out too much to enjoy it.

Fast Fish Tacos *by Lori Lange,* recipegirl.com

In Southern California, fish tacos are pretty much daily fare. You'll find them in all kinds of restaurants prepared in a variety of ways. Here's a fresh and healthy way to prepare fish tacos, and it will take you only about 20 minutes to get them on the table.

You can use any flaky white fish instead of tilapia, plain yogurt in place of sour cream, and shredded lettuce instead of cabbage. *Serves 4*

Preheat the broiler. Line a rimmed baking sheet with foil and place the tilapia pieces on the prepared baking sheet. Drizzle the fish with the oil and season to taste with salt and pepper. Broil the fish until it is golden-brown and flakes easily with a fork, 5 to 10 minutes. Remove from the oven.

While the fish is cooking, place the sour cream and 2 tablespoons of the salsa in a small bowl and stir to combine.

Divide the fish evenly among the taco shells and top with the cabbage, sour cream mixture, remaining salsa, and the avocado. Serve the fish tacos immediately with the lime wedges.

1 pound skinless tilapia fillets, cut into 2-inch pieces
1½ tablespoons olive oil
Salt and freshly ground black pepper
¾ cup light sour cream
¾ cup plus 2 tablespoons salsa, divided
4 large taco shells
1½ cups shredded cabbage
1 large avocado, peeled, pitted, and diced
1 lime, sliced into wedges

MAKE IT EASY
If you like, you can warm the taco shells while preparing the fish. Place them on a baking sheet on a lower rack in the oven while the fish is broiling. When the fish is done, your taco shells will be warmed and ready to fill.

Sweet & Crispy Chili Tilapia
by *Jenny Flake*, picky-palate.com

This sweet and salty recipe makes for a mouthwatering fish dinner. Find panko at Asian markets or in the Asian foods section of the supermarket. We love to eat this with a side of steamed broccoli.

Serves 4

Place the honey, water, and ¼ teaspoon of the chili powder in a small bowl; whisk to combine and set the honey glaze aside.

Place the panko, kosher salt, pepper, and remaining ½ teaspoon chili powder in a shallow dish and stir to combine. Season both sides of the tilapia fillets with pinches of kosher salt and pepper. Brush both sides of each tilapia fillet with the honey glaze, then press each fillet gently into the crumb mix, turning to coat both sides.

Heat the oil in a large skillet over medium heat. Add the panko-crusted tilapia fillets and cook until the crust is golden-brown and the fish flakes easily with a fork, about 3 minutes per side. Remove from the heat and serve warm.

3 tablespoons honey

2 teaspoons water

¾ teaspoon chili powder, divided

1½ cups panko (Japanese breadcrumbs)

½ teaspoon kosher salt, plus additional for seasoning

¼ teaspoon freshly ground black pepper, plus additional for seasoning

4 skinless tilapia fillets

2 tablespoons extra-virgin olive oil

Seafood

153

Mango & Clementine Salmon
by Rachel Rappaport, coconutandlime.com

1 medium onion, thinly sliced

1 2½-pound skin-on salmon fillet

1 large ripe mango, peeled and cut into ⅛-inch strips

3 Thai chiles, sliced

¼ cup fresh clementine juice

2½ tablespoons coconut vinegar
    Salt and freshly ground black pepper

1½ tablespoons olive oil

Super-delicious meets super-easy in this recipe. The cooking method is virtually foolproof; just take care to make sure the foil packet is sealed tightly so none of the lovely juices seep out. The clementine juice, mango, and chiles form a light, fruity, slightly spicy sauce as the salmon cooks. Coconut vinegar is a Filipino ingredient available in Asian markets. If you can't find coconut vinegar, try using apple cider vinegar instead. *Serves 6 to 8*

Preheat the oven to 350°F. Place a length of foil (about twice the length of the salmon) on a baking sheet. Place the onion slices in a single layer on half of the foil, creating a bed for the fish. Place the salmon fillet, skin side down, on the onion slices. Layer the mango strips on the salmon and top with the chile slices. Pour the clementine juice and coconut vinegar over the fish. Season to taste with salt and pepper and drizzle with the oil.

Fold the foil over and crimp it closed on all sides. Bake until the salmon is fully cooked and opaque in the center, about 20 minutes. Serve immediately.

MAKE IT EASY
Substitute low-pulp bottled orange or tangerine juice for the fresh clementine juice.

Pan-Roasted Sea Bass with Spiced Broccoli Rabe & Penne Rigate *by Laura Levy,* laurasbestrecipes.com

Chilean sea bass is also known as Patagonian toothfish. To avoid high mercury levels, be sure to purchase the fish from a reputable fishmonger; ask if it is certified by the Marine Stewardship Council, which indicates that the fisheries are sustainable and environmentally conscious. *Serves 4*

Preheat the oven to 400°F. Prepare the pasta according to the package instructions.

While the pasta is cooking, heat 1 tablespoon of the oil in a large skillet over medium-high heat. Add the garlic and broccoli rabe and cook, stirring frequently, until the broccoli rabe begins to brown, about 3 minutes. Add the red pepper flakes and lemon juice and cook, stirring, until the broccoli rabe is tender, about 2 minutes. Transfer the broccoli rabe mixture to a large serving bowl. Add the cooked pasta and toss to combine.

Season both sides of each sea bass fillet to taste with salt and black pepper. Heat the remaining 3 tablespoons oil in a large ovenproof skillet over medium-high heat until the oil shimmers and begins to smoke. Add the sea bass fillets and cook until lightly golden and caramelized, about 4 minutes per side. Transfer the skillet to the oven and bake until the fish is fully cooked and flakes easily with a fork, 3 minutes. Remove from the oven and let the fish rest for 2 minutes. Serve the sea bass with the prepared broccoli rabe and penne.

- 12 ounces penne rigate
- ¼ cup extra-virgin olive oil, divided
- 4 garlic cloves, diced
- 2 small bunches broccoli rabe, coarsely chopped
- ¼ teaspoon red pepper flakes
- ¼ cup fresh Meyer lemon juice
- 4 6-ounce Chilean sea bass fillets, 2½ inches thick
  Salt and freshly ground black pepper

MAKE IT EASY
No Meyer lemons? Use red wine vinegar instead of Meyer lemon juice in this recipe.

"Serving seafood on weeknights is a great, fast way to get dinner on the table. I love how healthy, fresh, and versatile seafood is and how easy it makes experimenting with new flavors."

–Laura Levy

Spicy Shrimp Salad *by Andrea Meyers,* andreasrecipes.com

- ¼ cup light olive oil
- ¾ pound medium shrimp, peeled and deveined
- 2 tablespoons chili powder
- ⅛ teaspoon sea salt, or to taste
- 1 small head lettuce, shredded
- 1 avocado, peeled, pitted, and cut into small chunks
- 1 lime, cut into wedges

Shrimp is excellent for quick meals because it needs just a little time to cook, and you can flavor it in many ways using different spices. For an even faster meal, simply thaw some cooked frozen shrimp and cut the shrimp's cooking time to two to three minutes. Shrimp needs room in a pan to cook properly, so if you don't have a large skillet, cook the shrimp in two batches. *Serves 4*

Heat the oil in a large skillet over medium-high heat. Add the shrimp and cook, stirring, until pink, about 4 minutes. Add the chili powder and sea salt and cook, stirring, for 1 to 2 more minutes. Remove from the heat.

Divide the lettuce among 4 large salad bowls and top with the avocado chunks. Divide the cooked shrimp among the bowls, then top each with 1 tablespoon of the chili oil from the skillet and squeeze a couple of the lime wedges over each salad. Serve immediately.

Crab & Avocado Omelet
by Shauna James Ahern and Daniel Ahern, glutenfreegirl.com

You might be intimidated by omelets. Time to get over that. This technique, while not the classic one, makes omelets much easier to create. Don't worry about making them look perfect. With crab and avocado inside, who is going to care if the omelet looks a little ragged? *Serves 4*

Preheat the broiler. Beat the eggs in a large bowl and season with the kosher salt and pepper.

Heat ½ tablespoon of the oil and ½ tablespoon of the butter in a large oven-proof pan over medium heat. When the butter is melted and begins to bubble, add half the egg mixture and cook, swirling the pan and using a spatula to scrape down the edges, until the eggs begin to set, 3 to 4 minutes. Transfer the skillet to the broiler and broil until the eggs are set but are not completely hardened, 30 seconds to 1 minute. Remove the pan from the oven.

Place ½ cup of the crabmeat and half of the avocado chunks on top of the cooked eggs. Slide a large spatula under the omelet to loosen it from the pan. Fold the omelet in half and transfer to a platter; cover it to keep warm.

Repeat with the remaining ingredients to make a second omelet. Cut each omelet in half and serve.

8 large eggs
2 teaspoons kosher salt
2 teaspoons freshly ground black pepper
1 tablespoon canola oil, divided
1 tablespoon unsalted butter, divided
1 cup cooked crabmeat, divided
1 ripe avocado, peeled, pitted, and cut into chunks

Pan-Fried Trout with Summer Vegetables

by Laura Levy, **laurasbestrecipes.com**

- 4 **8-ounce whole brook or rainbow trout, cleaned and boned with heads and tails intact**
- 12 **fresh basil leaves plus 6 thinly sliced fresh basil leaves, divided**
- 12 **sprigs fresh Italian parsley**
  Salt and freshly ground black pepper
- 4 **tablespoons olive oil**
- 6 **garlic cloves, peeled and thinly sliced**
- 5 **small plum tomatoes, seeded and chopped**
- 2 **medium zucchini, trimmed and chopped**
- 1 **cup frozen petit yellow corn kernels**

This recipe is wonderful on a summer night. It doesn't take long to prepare but will appear as if you spent a lot of time on it. When I have friends over for dinner on a busy weeknight, I prepare this and usually get a lot of oohs and ahhs because it's so colorful and fresh looking. This is one of my go-to dishes when I want to make something special but don't have a lot of time.

Use two skillets to cook this quickly, or cook it in two batches, keeping the first batch in a warm oven until ready to serve. *Serves 4*

Rinse the trout and thoroughly dry inside and out with paper towels. Fill each trout cavity with 3 basil leaves and 3 parsley sprigs. Using kitchen twine, tie each trout cavity closed. Season each trout to taste with salt and pepper.

Place 2 large skillets over high heat and heat 2 tablespoons of the oil in each skillet until the oil begins to shimmer. Add half of the garlic to each skillet and cook, stirring, for about 3 minutes. Remove the garlic from the oil and discard.

Place 2 trout in each skillet and cook until browned and slightly crisp, 3 to 4 minutes per side. Reduce the heat to low and add half of the tomatoes, half of the zucchini, half of the corn, and half of the sliced basil to each skillet. Simmer until the vegetables are cooked but still firm and the fish flakes easily with a fork, 8 to 10 minutes. Transfer the cooked fish and vegetables to a platter and serve immediately.

Panko-Crusted Shrimp with Orange-Almond Rice & Spinach *by Lori Lange*, **recipegirl.com**

This recipe has become what is affectionately known as a "major keeper" in our house. The coating of breadcrumbs is just enough to give the shrimp a bit of crunch when they are lightly fried in oil, and the rice packs enough flavors to carry the rest of the dish. Served over fresh spinach leaves, this dinner is both healthy and delicious. *Serves 4*

Bring the chicken broth and orange juice to a boil in a medium saucepan over medium-high heat. Add the rice and cook according to the package instructions. Add the almonds, stir, and season to taste with salt.

While the rice is cooking, place the shrimp and egg whites in a medium bowl and toss to coat. Place the panko, parsley, and pepper in a large resealable plastic bag and shake to combine. Add the shrimp to the bag and shake to coat the shrimp.

Heat the oil in a large skillet over medium-high heat. Place the shrimp in the skillet in a single layer and cook until golden-brown, about 3 minutes per side. Divide the spinach among 4 plates. Top each with the hot cooked rice and 6 cooked shrimp. Serve immediately.

1½ cups chicken broth
½ cup orange juice
1 cup uncooked long-grain white rice
2 tablespoons sliced almonds, toasted
Salt
24 jumbo shrimp, peeled and deveined
2 large egg whites, lightly beaten
¾ cup panko (Japanese breadcrumbs)
2 tablespoons chopped fresh Italian parsley
⅛ teaspoon freshly ground black pepper
1 tablespoon olive oil
2 cups (packed) spinach leaves

MAKE IT EASY
Use quick-cooking rice that cooks in under 10 minutes and you'll have this dinner on the table in about 20 minutes!

Seafood

161

Halibut Pesto Kabobs *by Catherine McCord,* **weelicious.com**

FOR PESTO:
- 2 **cups fresh basil leaves**
- ¼ **cup freshly grated Parmesan cheese**
- ¼ **cup pine nuts**
- 1 **garlic clove, peeled**
- ½ **teaspoon salt**
- ¼ **cup olive oil**

FOR KABOBS:
- 1 **pound halibut, cut into 1-inch cubes**
- 1 **cup cherry tomatoes**
- 2 **bell peppers, stemmed, seeded, and cut into wedges**

This is easily one of my favorite healthy recipes and everyone in our family enjoys it. For this recipe, my son, Kenya, and I love going out into the garden to pick our ingredients, returning to the kitchen to whip up the pesto and skewer up the kabobs, and then heading out to the grill to cook up this delicious entrée. *Serves 4*

For Pesto: Place all the pesto ingredients in a food processor and puree until smooth. Set aside.

For Kabobs: Prepare the grill to high or preheat the broiler. Place all the kabob ingredients in a large bowl, add ½ cup of the pesto, and toss gently. Thread the fish and vegetables onto skewers (if using bamboo skewers, soak them in water for 30 minutes beforehand to avoid burning them on the grill). Grill the kabobs, turning once, until the fish is golden and firm to the touch, about 3 minutes per side. Serve the kabobs with the remaining pesto.

Good Bite Weeknight Meals: Delicious Made Easy

MAKE IT EASY
To save time, do your prep the night before, then just bring the halibut kabobs to room temperature before grilling.

Broiled Salmon with Hoisin Glaze

by Andrea Meyers, **andreasrecipes.com**

2 tablespoons hoisin sauce

2 tablespoons orange marmalade

½ teaspoon grated fresh ginger
  Nonstick cooking spray

4 6-ounce skinless salmon fillets,
  1 inch thick
  Salt and freshly ground black
  pepper

Hoisin sauce is a Chinese condiment with salty, sweet, and spicy flavors and it is often used as a glaze for meats. The orange and ginger in this glaze balance the savory hoisin without making it overly sweet. While preparing the salmon, you can stir-fry some vegetables or toss a quick salad to go along with it. *Serves 4*

Preheat the broiler. Place the hoisin sauce, marmalade, and ginger in a small bowl and stir to combine. Set the hoisin mixture aside.

Line a baking sheet with foil and spray the foil with nonstick cooking spray. Brush both sides of each salmon fillet with the hoisin mixture and place the salmon fillets on the prepared baking sheet. Season each fillet with salt and pepper.

Broil the salmon until the sides of the fillets are golden and the fish flakes easily with a fork, 8 to 10 minutes. Remove the salmon from the oven, let it cool for 1 to 2 minutes, then serve.

Curried Shrimp Fried Rice

by Julie Van Rosendaal, **dinnerwithjulie.com**

Fried rice is the ultimate in healthy fast food. Leftover rice is ideal to start with—once cold, the grains separate and won't clump together as you fry them. Fried rice also makes use of any number of leftovers—scraps of roast chicken or pork and raw or cooked vegetables always seem to work. If there's nothing else in the fridge, crack in an egg and scramble it off to the side as the rice cooks. Using brown rice will boost fiber and provide other nutrients, such as B vitamins and iron. *Serves 4*

Heat the oil in a large skillet over medium-high heat. Add the cold rice, peas, and curry paste or powder. Cook until the rice begins to turn golden and sizzle, about 5 minutes.

Using a spatula, push the rice to one side of the skillet and crack the eggs into the other side; scramble the eggs as they cook, then stir them into the rice. Add the shrimp and scallions and cook until the shrimp are pink and opaque, about 3 minutes. Season with the soy sauce and serve immediately.

1 tablespoon canola or olive oil

2 cups cold cooked long-grain white or brown rice

½ cup frozen peas, thawed

2 teaspoons curry paste or powder

2 large eggs

½ pound shrimp, peeled and deveined

2 scallions, thinly sliced

1 to 2 tablespoons soy sauce, or to taste

Confetti Shrimp & Grits
by Kath Younger, katheats.com

Shrimp and grits is one of those magical, soul-warming combinations. In this recipe, the creamy corn polenta provides a base for colorful peppers and fresh local shrimp. Touches of honey and butter add the slightest bit of rich sweetness. *Serves 4*

Heat 1 tablespoon of the oil in a large pan over medium heat. Place the shrimp in a single layer in the pan, cooking until golden and crisp, about 5 minutes per side. Remove the shrimp from the pan and set aside.

Add the remaining 1 tablespoon oil, the carrots, bell pepper, and celery to the pan and cook, stirring, until softened, about 5 minutes. Add the Old Bay seasoning, chili powder, and water and stir gently to deglaze the pan. Cook until the vegetables are tender, 2 to 3 more minutes. Remove the vegetables from the pan and set aside, reserving the liquid in the pan.

Add the broccoli rabe to the pan and cook, stirring and adding additional water if needed, until wilted, about 5 minutes. Remove the broccoli rabe, drain, and set aside with the other cooked vegetables.

While the broccoli rabe is cooking, prepare the polenta according to the package instructions. When the polenta is cooked, add the butter and stir until the butter is melted; add the honey and stir gently. Add the cooked vegetables to the polenta and stir. To serve, top the polenta with the cooked shrimp and the cheese.

2 tablespoons olive oil, divided
36 to 48 medium shrimp, peeled, deveined, and tails removed
2 medium carrots, peeled and diced
1 large red bell pepper, stemmed, seeded, and diced
2 celery stalks, diced
2 teaspoons Old Bay seasoning
¼ teaspoon chili powder
⅓ cup water
1 small bunch broccoli rabe, chopped
½ cup quick-cooking polenta
2 tablespoons unsalted butter
1 tablespoon honey
Freshly grated Parmesan cheese

MAKE IT EASY
No broccoli rabe? Spinach or other greens will work in this recipe, too.

Seafood

167

Cilantro-Garlic Prawn Skewers with Avocado-Mango Jasmine Rice

by Laura Levy, laurasbestrecipes.com

½ cup olive oil

5 garlic cloves, minced

3 tablespoons fresh lime juice

2 tablespoons minced fresh ginger

6 tablespoons chopped fresh cilantro leaves, divided

2 pounds pink or jumbo white prawns, peeled and deveined

2 cups uncooked jasmine rice

2 avocados, peeled, pitted, and cut into small chunks

2 ripe mangoes, peeled, pitted, and cut into ½-inch cubes

½ yellow bell pepper, stemmed, seeded, and finely diced

Salt and freshly ground black pepper

I like to use wild prawns and avoid the farmed variety. To give your rice a little kick, you can "scent" it by adding 1 to 2 teaspoons orange zest or Meyer lemon zest to the water while the rice is cooking. For extra spice, add half a chopped serrano chile to the marinade. *Serves 4*

Prepare the grill to medium-high. Place the oil, garlic, lime juice, ginger, and 3 tablespoons of the cilantro in a large resealable plastic bag and shake to combine. Add the prawns to the bag and marinate for 20 minutes. (If necessary, use 2 bags or a large baking dish instead.)

Prepare the jasmine rice according to the package instructions. When the rice is cooked, add the avocados and mangoes, bell pepper, and remaining 3 tablespoons cilantro, tossing gently to combine. Season to taste with salt and black pepper.

Thread the prawns on metal skewers and grill until the prawns are opaque and lightly charred, about 3 minutes per side. Serve immediately with the avocado-mango rice.

Parmesan-Crusted Fish with Lemon-Dill Sauce *by Catherine McCord,* weelicious.com

When my son, Kenya, was around 10 months old, I started placing tiny pieces of fish on his high-chair tray for him to pick up and eat on his own. When my daughter, Chloe, was around the same age, I did it with her as well. And like her older brother, Chloe is a fish fanatic.

Fish is an important source of protein and other of nutrients for kids, like B vitamins and omega-3s, but there are many children who just plain ol' resist eating it. This recipe is for those parents whose little ones put up a fight on fish night. As soon as your kids take a bite of this Parmesan-crusted fish, I bet they'll change their tune. I even added a delicious lemon-dill dipping sauce to get them more involved with the dish and add to the fun factor of eating it. You never know—your kids may be requesting fish after this! *Serves 4*

Preheat the oven to 400°F. Place the cheese, breadcrumbs, and ½ teaspoon of the salt in a shallow bowl or on a plate and stir to combine. Press both sides of each fish fillet in the breadcrumb mixture to coat.

Spray a baking rack with nonstick cooking spray and place it on a baking sheet. Spray each fish fillet with cooking spray and place the fillets on the baking rack. Bake the fish until the crust is golden and the fish is fully cooked and flakes easily with a fork, 12 to 15 minutes.

While the fish is baking, place the yogurt, lemon juice, dill, and remaining ¼ teaspoon salt in a medium bowl and stir to combine. Serve the fish fillets with the lemon-dill sauce.

¼ cup freshly grated Parmesan cheese
¼ cup breadcrumbs
¾ teaspoon salt, divided
4 skinless fish fillets (such as tilapia, red snapper, halibut, or any other white, flaky fish)
Nonstick cooking spray
½ cup plain yogurt
2 tablespoons fresh lemon juice
2 teaspoons chopped fresh dill or 1 teaspoon dried dill

MAKE IT EASY
Make a double batch of the sauce to serve with vegetables. If you'd like to freeze the uncooked fillets, place them on a baking sheet after breading them, freeze them for 1 hour, place them in a large resealable plastic bag, and store them in the freezer for up to 4 months.

Shrimp & Sea Bass Ceviche Salad

by Laura Levy, laurasbestrecipes.com

- 2 **pounds shrimp, peeled, deveined, tails removed, and cut into ½-inch pieces**
- 1 **pound sea bass fillets, cut into ½-inch cubes**
- 8 **tablespoons fresh lime juice, plus 1 lime cut into wedges for garnish**
- 3 **tablespoons fresh lemon juice**
- 2 **medium tomatoes, diced**
- 1 **small white onion, finely chopped**
- 1 **small yellow bell pepper, stemmed, seeded, and chopped**
- 1 **small red bell pepper, stemmed, seeded, and chopped**
- 2 **to 3 jalapeño or serrano chiles, stemmed, seeded, and finely chopped**
- ¾ **cup chopped fresh cilantro leaves, plus additional cilantro leaves for garnish**
- 1 **teaspoon olive oil, plus additional for drizzling**
- 4 **cups chopped romaine lettuce, chilled**
- **Sea salt and freshly ground black pepper**
- 2 **avocados, peeled, pitted, and thinly sliced, for garnish**

In ceviche, seafood is denatured, or "cooked," by citrus. To make this recipe easier, you can marinate the fish and shrimp up to 24 hours in advance, then add everything else just before you're ready to serve. *Serves 4*

Place the shrimp and sea bass pieces in a large glass or ceramic bowl. Add the lime juice and lemon juice and toss gently. Cover and marinate in the refrigerator until the shrimp and fish are opaque, at least 1 hour, then drain.

Place the tomatoes, onion, bell peppers, chiles, cilantro, and oil in another large bowl and toss to combine. Add the ceviche and toss gently.

To serve, divide the lettuce among 4 plates; drizzle with olive oil and season to taste with sea salt and black pepper. Top each bed of lettuce with the ceviche and garnish with avocado slices, lime wedges, and a few cilantro leaves.

MAKE IT EASY
To chill the lettuce leaves, place them in the freezer for 10 minutes.

FIVE

Pasta

One-Pot, Stove-Top Macaroni & Cheese

by Todd Porter and Diane Cu, **whiteonricecouple.com**

There's nothing more satisfying than a nice big bowl of decadent, cheesy pasta, and that's exactly what this macaroni and cheese recipe delivers. There's no oven required, and you can choose any cheese you like, though if you pick a hard cheese you'll want to combine it with something that melts easily.

Stir this macaroni and cheese constantly as you cook it, to keep the macaroni from clumping together or sticking to the pot. *Serves 4*

Rinse and drain the macaroni in a colander. Place the macaroni, milk, butter, salt, mustard, and nutmeg in a medium saucepan over medium heat and bring to a simmer, stirring frequently, about 5 minutes. Reduce the heat to low and cook, stirring frequently and adding more milk if needed, until the macaroni has absorbed the milk and is fully cooked, 15 to 20 more minutes.

Add the cheese, stir, and remove from the heat. Sprinkle the breadcrumbs, if using, evenly over the macaroni and cheese, cover, and let the mixture rest until the macaroni has plumped and absorbed any excess milk, about 10 minutes. Season to taste with salt and stir before serving.

2 cups large elbow macaroni
1½ cups low-fat milk
1 tablespoon unsalted butter
1 teaspoon salt
½ teaspoon mustard powder
⅛ teaspoon freshly grated nutmeg
1 cup grated cheese (see Headnote)
Breadcrumbs (optional)

MAKE IT EASY
If you don't have whole nutmeg on hand, substitute ground nutmeg.

Broccoli & Garlic Pasta

by Rachel Rappaport, coconutandlime.com

- 10 ounces pasta
- 3 tablespoons olive oil
- 3 garlic cloves, chopped
- 1 shallot, chopped
- 1 tablespoon minced fresh oregano
  Salt and freshly ground black pepper
- 2 heads broccoli, cut into florets
- ¾ cup breadcrumbs

The toasty flavor of the breadcrumbs makes this dish stand out. Use homemade breadcrumbs or store-bought; either will be delicious. You can also use any pasta you like in this recipe. *Serves 4*

Prepare the pasta according to the package instructions.

While the pasta is cooking, heat the oil in a large pan over medium-high heat. Add the garlic, shallot, and oregano and season to taste with salt and pepper. Cook until fragrant, 2 to 3 minutes. Add the broccoli and cook, stirring occasionally, until the broccoli is almost tender, about 6 minutes. Add the breadcrumbs and cook, stirring gently to combine, until hot, 2 to 3 minutes. Add the hot cooked pasta and toss gently. Serve immediately.

MAKE IT EASY
Use packaged precut broccoli florets or broccoli crowns, which frequently need only a single chop to break into florets.

Fresh Tomatoes & Capellini
by Matt Armendariz, **mattbites.com**

I'm crazy about this simple, summery dish. It's easy to prepare, as the tomatoes need not be cooked, but be forewarned: you'll need the best possible tomatoes you can find. And if that means waiting to create this dish, so be it! This dish is great as is, but you can also top it with a bit of high-quality canned tuna, if you like. *Serves 4*

Core and roughly chop one-third of the assorted tomatoes. Cut the remaining assorted tomatoes in half and rub the cut sides against the large holes of a box grater. Grate the cut tomatoes into a large bowl, saving the pulp and discarding the skin. Place the tomato pulp, chopped tomatoes, cherry tomatoes, lemon juice, garlic, sea salt, and pepper in a large serving bowl, tossing to combine. Let the tomato sauce rest until ready to use, at least 10 minutes.

While the tomato sauce rests, prepare the pasta according to the package instructions. Drain the pasta, add it to the tomato sauce, and toss well. Add the basil and oil and season to taste with sea salt. Serve immediately.

2 pounds assorted ripe tomatoes, divided
1 pound cherry tomatoes, quartered
2½ tablespoons fresh lemon juice
1 garlic clove, finely chopped
1 teaspoon sea salt, plus additional for seasoning
½ teaspoon freshly ground black pepper
1 pound capellini
½ cup chopped fresh basil leaves
1 to 2 tablespoons extra-virgin olive oil

"Less time doesn't have to mean less flavor. Some of my favorite go-to recipes are simple and quick, including this pasta that features kabocha."

—*Marc Matsumoto*

Slow-Cooker Lasagne *by Christy Jordan,* **southernplate.com**

1 pound cottage cheese

2 cups shredded mozzarella cheese

2 26-ounce jars pasta sauce

2 pounds lean ground beef, cooked

1 9-ounce package lasagna noodles

Lasagne used to be a time-consuming dinner at my house until I developed this recipe. We eat half and freeze the other half for another busy day. There is nothing like coming home at the end of a long day and having dinner at the ready! *Serves 8*

Place the cottage cheese and mozzarella cheese in a medium bowl and stir to combine.

Add a thin layer of the pasta sauce to the bottom of a slow cooker. Add a thin layer of the cooked ground beef and a layer of the noodles, breaking the noodles to make them fit. Top the noodle layer with a layer of the cheese mixture. Repeat until all the ingredients are used, alternating the direction of the noodles with each layer and ending with a layer of sauce. Cover and cook on low for 6 to 8 hours. Serve hot.

Christy Jordan, southernplate.com

Christy Jordan publishes Southern Plate (southernplate.com), a website dedicated to teaching and preserving classic Southern foods. She holds a BS degree in home economics. Jordan is a mother of two and lives with her husband in North Alabama, where her family has resided for the past nine generations. Her style of cooking is no-fuss Southern classic because, as she says, "At the end of the day, I think what folks really want is to come home to food like Granny made, prepared by someone who loves them." Christy Jordan's first cookbook, *Southern Plate: Classic Comfort Food That Makes Everyone Feel Like Family*, was published by HarperCollins in 2010.

More About Christy

What do you always have in your shopping cart?
Self-rising flour. So many of our Southern recipes revolve around this and I seem to be forever running out!

What's your go-to weeknight dinner?
My go-to weeknight meal is "something on a biscuit." On those nights when the kids have activities or we are all pulled in different directions, I can whip up a batch of biscuits and fry some pork chops or heat up leftover ham to go on them and we can all have supper on the go. They're easy, filling, and the old-fashioned version of fast food.

What's your favorite kitchen tool?
My hands. I don't buy into the whole kitchen tool craze. My grandmothers made almost everything using a simple mixing bowl, a wooden spoon, and their hands.

Is there anything you just can't eat?
I've never eaten seafood and neither has anyone in my family. My ancestors were mountain people, so seafood was not readily available to them. As a result we're generations into a family who sticks to the farm and land when it comes to our diets!

Ramp & Scallop Linguine *by Marc Matsumoto,* **norecipes.com**

8 ounces linguine

3 tablespoons extra-virgin olive oil

½ pound trimmed dry sea scallops, each cut into 3 slices (see Headnote)

½ pound ramps, roughly chopped

Red pepper flakes (optional)

Salt and freshly ground black pepper

1 lemon, cut into wedges

This is one of my favorite springtime pastas. Because of its simplicity, each component of this dish has a starring role. The firm, sweet scallops and garlicky ramps play together nicely while providing just a bit of tasty liquid that flavors the pasta.

If you can't find ramps in your area, use garlic chives or garlic scapes. As for the scallops, look for scallops that are sold "dry." This means they haven't been chemically treated to retain more moisture, which has a tendency to make them soft and mushy. Serve the pasta with a wedge of lemon to add a little brightness. *Serves 4*

Prepare the pasta in a large pot according to the package instructions. Drain the pasta and set aside.

Heat the oil in the same pot over high heat until it shimmers. Add the scallops and stir-fry until slightly opaque, about 30 seconds. Add the ramps and stir-fry until bright green, about 1 minute. Remove the pot from the heat and add the red pepper flakes, if desired, and the cooked pasta. Season to taste with salt and black pepper and toss. Serve immediately with the lemon wedges.

Pork Ragu *by Jaden Hair,* **steamykitchen.com**

Serve this hearty, stewlike sauce over the pasta of your choice for a delicious, no-fuss, weeknight meal. Using ground pork adds an interesting twist to a classic recipe, and the ragu makes great leftovers. *Serves 4 to 6*

Prepare the pasta according to the package instructions.

While the pasta is cooking, heat the oil in a large pot over medium heat. Add the onion and cook, stirring, for 30 seconds. Add the garlic and cook, stirring, for 30 seconds. Add the bell pepper and carrot and cook until the vegetables are softened and golden-brown, stirring occasionally, about 5 minutes.

Increase the heat to high and add the ground pork, using a spatula or spoon to break up the meat. Cook until the pork is browned, about 5 minutes. Add the crushed tomatoes, balsamic vinegar, kosher salt, and sugar and bring to a boil, about 5 minutes. Reduce the heat to low, cover, and simmer, stirring occasionally, for 45 minutes. Serve over the hot cooked pasta.

1   **pound pasta**
2   **tablespoons olive oil**
1   **small onion, diced**
3   **garlic cloves, minced**
1   **bell pepper, stemmed, seeded, and diced**
1   **large carrot, peeled and diced**
1   **pound lean ground pork**
1   **28-ounce can crushed tomatoes**
1½ **tablespoons balsamic vinegar**
1½ **teaspoons kosher salt**
1   **teaspoon sugar**

MAKE IT EASY
Don't have a lot of time to let the ragu simmer? Cooking it for the full 45 minutes will help the flavors meld, but you can let the ragu simmer for as little as 15 minutes.

Mushroom Ravioli with Garlic-Sage Brown Butter & Asparagus *by Kate Jones,* ourbestbites.com

This meal is elegant enough for dinner guests, but it's so quick and easy that you can make it for the family any weeknight after work. If you're not crazy about mushroom ravioli, use cheese, beef, or chicken ravioli instead—just be careful that your choice of ravioli doesn't overwhelm the delicate flavor of the brown butter and sage. *Serves 4*

Prepare the ravioli according to the package instructions.

While the ravioli is cooking, heat the oil in a large skillet over medium-high heat. Add the asparagus and cook until crisp-tender, about 3 minutes. Season to taste with salt and pepper. Remove from the heat and cover to keep warm.

Melt the butter in a small skillet over medium-high heat, stirring frequently, until light brown and fragrant, about 4 minutes. Add the garlic and sage and cook, stirring, until the garlic is fragrant, about 1 minute. Remove from the heat. Add the cooked ravioli, brown butter sauce, and asparagus to a large bowl, tossing gently to coat. Season to taste with salt and pepper and serve immediately.

2　8-ounce packages mushroom ravioli
1½　tablespoons olive oil
1　pound asparagus, trimmed and cut into 1½-inch pieces
　Salt and freshly ground black pepper
4　tablespoons (½ stick) butter
8　garlic cloves, minced
¼　cup chopped fresh sage

Pasta Carbonara *by Matt Armendariz,* **mattbites.com**

- **1 pound bucatini or spaghetti**
- **½ pound bacon, chopped**
- **½ tablespoon chopped garlic**
  Salt and freshly ground black pepper
- **4 large eggs, beaten well**
- **1 cup freshly grated Parmigiano-Reggiano or pecorino cheese, divided**
- **1½ tablespoons chopped fresh Italian parsley**

This recipe is rich, silky, and savory. When it comes to decadent pastas, pasta carbonara is top-notch in my book! It's all about the technique here, folks; you must add the eggs to the pasta when it's not on direct heat so that the eggs don't scramble. The pasta will still be warm enough to cook the eggs, which results in a creamy sauce. *Serves 4*

Prepare the pasta according to the package instructions.

While the pasta is cooking, place the chopped bacon in a large sauté pan over medium heat and cook until crisp and browned, 3 to 5 minutes. Transfer the bacon to paper towels to drain. Drain the pan, reserving 2 to 3 tablespoons of bacon fat in the pan. Add the garlic to the pan and cook over medium heat for 30 seconds. Season to taste with pepper. Add the cooked pasta and cooked chopped bacon to the pan and cook for 1 minute. Remove the pan from the heat.

Season the beaten eggs to taste with salt. Add the eggs to the pan, tossing and folding gently so the eggs thicken but do not scramble. Add ½ cup of the cheese and stir, then transfer the mixture to a large serving bowl. Top with the remaining ½ cup cheese and the parsley. Serve immediately.

Pasta Primavera *by Lori Lange,* **recipegirl.com**

The light, creamy sauce in this pasta primavera comes together quite easily. Use plenty of your favorite fresh vegetables and you can add this to your healthy-eating menu. *Serves 4*

Prepare the pasta in a large pot according to the package instructions. In the last 2 minutes of cooking, add the vegetables to the boiling water. Cook until the vegetables are slightly tender, about 2 minutes. Drain the pasta and vegetables and return them to the pot.

While the pasta is cooking, heat the milk in a small saucepan over medium heat until just hot, 1 to 2 minutes. Remove from the heat and add the cheese and flour, whisking until smooth. Season the sauce to taste with salt and pepper.

Add the sauce to the pasta and vegetables and toss to coat. Serve the pasta primavera hot, with additional cheese.

12 ounces pasta (such as farfalle, penne, rigatoni, or tortellini)

3 cups mixed vegetables (broccoli, cauliflower, and red bell peppers)

1 cup canned low-fat evaporated milk, half-and-half, or 2% milk

⅔ cup freshly grated Parmesan cheese, plus additional for serving

1 tablespoon all-purpose flour
Salt and freshly ground black pepper

Greek Pasta Salad *by Kath Younger,* **katheats.com**

2 **cups whole wheat penne**
3 **cups chopped zucchini**
½ **cup chopped pitted kalamata olives**
¼ **pound feta cheese**
¼ **cup Greek salad dressing**

This simple pasta salad combines the flavors of salty kalamata olives and feta cheese to balance fresh zucchini and a tangy Greek dressing. It's good hot or cold; enjoy it at the dinner table or in your lunchbox the next day. *Serves 4*

Prepare the pasta in a large pot according to the package instructions. In the last 2 minutes of cooking, add the zucchini and cook for 2 minutes. Drain the pasta and zucchini and transfer to a large serving bowl. Add the olives, cheese, and salad dressing and toss to combine. Serve the pasta salad hot or cold.

Kath Younger, **katheats.com**

Kath Younger writes a popular healthy food blog read by more than 10,000 daily visitors worldwide. Kath Eats Real Food (katheats.com) features photos of Kath's meals, stories about her life, and the recipes she and her husband create. After losing more than 30 pounds since graduating from college, Kath became a registered dietitian. She runs a Great Harvest Bread Company with her husband in Charlottesville, Virginia.

More About Kath

What do you always have in your shopping cart?

I have a rule that I have to eat a tin of sardines each week—for nutrition. Calcium, vitamin D, omega-3—it's a nutrition trifecta! Plus, sardines are cheap and easy. Other items that are always in my shopping cart include milk and bananas for morning oatmeal, Greek yogurt for quick lunches, and salad ingredients such as spinach, bell pepper, broccoli, and carrots.

What's your go-to weeknight dinner?

My go-to weeknight dinner is eggs and toast, with something green on the side. Eggs are nutritious and take no time to cook. Sometimes I even microwave them in a ramekin for a no-clean-up-required poached egg. Being bakery owners, my husband and I always have great bread on hand. And as a nutritionist, I add something green, like sautéed bok choy or kale chips.

What's your favorite kitchen tool?

My salad spinner! I couldn't live without it. I use it almost once a day to prep salads and greens.

Is there anything you just can't eat?

You'll never see raw onions cross my lips. I have a very keen sense of smell and taste, and if I accidentally eat raw onion, I'll taste it with every breath for days. I don't like cooked onions either, but I just eat around them.

Orzo with Spinach & Peas
by Rachel Rappaport, coconutandlime.com

This one-pot vegetarian pasta dish is a wonderful alternative to risotto or traditional pasta dishes. Orzo cooks very quickly, so dinner can be ready in a matter of minutes. Try sprinkling any leftovers with lemon juice and serve it as cold salad for lunch. *Serves 4*

Place the oil, onion, and garlic in a large pot over medium heat and cook, stirring, until softened, about 5 minutes. Add the water and salt; increase the heat to high and bring to a boil. Add the orzo and cook for 5 minutes. Add the spinach, peas, and cheese and stir. Cover, reduce the heat to medium, and cook until the orzo is tender. Remove from the heat and season to taste with salt and pepper. Stir before serving.

2 tablespoons olive oil
1 small onion, chopped
1 garlic clove, chopped
2 cups water
½ teaspoon salt, plus additional for seasoning
1 pound orzo
1 cup (packed) roughly chopped spinach leaves
½ cup frozen peas
¼ cup freshly grated Parmesan cheese
   Freshly ground black pepper

MAKE IT EASY
Use frozen chopped spinach instead of fresh. Defrost it in seconds in the microwave; for this recipe, it can be added directly to the pot without draining.

Scallop & Artichoke Pasta

by Rachel Rappaport, coconutandlime.com

12 ounces pasta

3 tablespoons olive oil

1 small onion, diced

3 garlic cloves, minced

1 pound trimmed bay scallops

10 ounces frozen artichoke hearts, thawed

¼ cup fresh lemon juice

¼ cup chopped fresh Italian parsley

1 teaspoon lemon zest

½ cup toasted breadcrumbs

⅓ cup freshly grated Parmesan cheese

A dinner featuring scallops and artichokes sounds and tastes luxurious, but this recipe is simple enough to make on a weeknight. It is also quite thrifty; flavorful bay scallops are much more affordable than sea scallops, and frozen artichokes are a fraction of the price of fresh. *Serves 4*

Prepare the pasta according to the package instructions.

While the pasta is cooking, heat the oil in a large skillet over medium-high heat. Add the onion and garlic and cook, stirring, until just fragrant, 3 to 5 minutes. Stir in the scallops, artichokes, and lemon juice and cook until the scallops are almost opaque, about 5 minutes. Stir in the parsley and lemon zest and cook for 1 minute. Remove from the heat.

Place the pasta, scallop mixture, breadcrumbs, and cheese in a large bowl and toss gently. Serve hot.

MAKE IT EASY

If you don't want to keep a block of Parmesan cheese on hand, buy high-quality grated Parmesan cheese from an Italian market or the Italian foods section of the supermarket. It is much tastier than the stuff that comes in a can, but just as easy to use.

Chicken Parmesan & Rigatoni Bake

by Jenny Flake, **picky-palate.com**

This is a great weeknight dinner the whole family will love. To save time, I bake the chicken and pasta at the same time, then slice the chicken and layer it over the pasta right before serving. Serve this dinner with a fresh green salad and your favorite steamed vegetables.
Serves 6

Prepare the pasta according to the package instructions.

While the pasta is cooking, prepare the chicken. Preheat the oven to 350°F. Line a baking sheet with foil. Spray a baking rack with nonstick cooking spray and place it on the baking sheet. Place the flour, salt, and black pepper in a shallow dish and stir to combine. Place the eggs and water in a second shallow dish and beat lightly to combine. Place the Italian breadcrumbs, panko, and Parmesan cheese in a third shallow dish and stir to combine. Dredge both sides of the chicken breasts in the flour, then the egg mixture, and then the breadcrumb mixture, pressing gently to coat. Place the coated chicken breasts on the prepared baking rack and set aside.

Heat the oil in a large pot over medium heat. Add the onion and bell pepper and cook, stirring, until softened, about 5 minutes. Add the garlic and cook, stirring, for 1 minute. Add the pasta sauce. Reduce the heat to low, add the cooked pasta, and stir.

Spray a 9x13-inch baking dish with nonstick cooking spray. Transfer the pasta mixture to the prepared baking dish. Top with the mozzarella cheese.

Place the chicken and pasta in the oven. Bake until the chicken is golden-brown and fully cooked and the cheese on the pasta is melted and bubbling, 20 to 25 minutes. To serve, cut the chicken into strips and layer over the pasta.

- 1 pound rigatoni
  Nonstick cooking spray
- ½ cup all-purpose flour
- 1 teaspoon salt
- ½ teaspoon freshly ground black pepper
- 2 large eggs
- 2 tablespoons water
- ½ cup Italian breadcrumbs
- ½ cup panko (Japanese breadcrumbs)
- ½ cup freshly grated Parmesan cheese
- 4 large boneless skinless chicken breasts, pounded to a ½-inch thickness between two sheets of plastic wrap
- 2 tablespoons extra-virgin olive oil
- 1 medium onion, chopped
- 1 large red bell pepper, stemmed, seeded, and diced
- 3 garlic cloves, minced
- 2 26-ounce jars pasta sauce
- 1½ cups shredded mozzarella cheese

Zucchini & Mushroom Pasta with Lemon Basil *by Andrea Meyers,* **andreasrecipes.com**

1 **pound farfalle (bow-tie pasta)**
3 **tablespoons olive oil**
3 **shallots, thinly sliced**
4 **garlic cloves, minced**
½ **pound cremini mushrooms, thinly sliced**
2 **medium zucchini, sliced**
½ **cup (packed) fresh lemon basil leaves, cut into thin strips**
1 **cup dry white wine**
¼ **cup freshly grated Parmesan cheese**

Lemon basil is a fragrant and slightly sweet variety that adds bright lemon flavor to salads and chicken and fish dishes. This light pasta dish is a showcase for summery zucchini and lemon basil and has just enough mushrooms to make it filling. If fresh lemon basil isn't available at your local market, you can substitute regular fresh basil and add a little lemon juice. *Serves 4*

Prepare the pasta in a large pot according to the package instructions.

While the pasta is cooking, heat the oil in a large skillet over medium heat. Add the shallots and garlic and cook, stirring, until the shallots are wilted and limp, about 3 minutes. Add the mushrooms and cook, stirring, for 2 more minutes. Add the zucchini and cook, stirring, until the zucchini are softened, about 4 minutes.

Add the basil and wine and cook until the wine is reduced to half of its original volume, about 7 minutes. Add the cheese, stir, and cook for 2 more minutes. Toss the zucchini mixture with the cooked pasta in a large bowl and serve.

Shrimp & Pasta Salad *by Rachel Rappaport, coconutandlime.com*

Here in Baltimore, we put Old Bay seasoning on everything! One of the best uses of it is in this shrimp and pasta salad. On its own, shrimp salad isn't quite a full meal, but the pasta makes it substantial enough to have for lunch or dinner. You can use whichever type of small pasta you like in this recipe. *Serves 4*

Prepare the pasta according to the package instructions.

While the pasta is cooking, place the mayonnaise, Old Bay seasoning, salt, and pepper in a small bowl and whisk to combine. Set the dressing aside.

Place the cooked pasta, steamed shrimp, and celery in a large bowl. Add the dressing and toss to coat. Serve warm or cold.

½ pound small pasta
¼ cup mayonnaise
1 tablespoon Old Bay seasoning
¼ teaspoon salt
½ teaspoon freshly ground black pepper
1½ pounds shrimp, peeled, deveined, and steamed
1 celery stalk, diced

MAKE IT EASY
Have your fishmonger steam the shrimp for you.

Kabocha & Brown Butter Pasta

by Marc Matsumoto, norecipes.com

½ pound pasta (such as
    pappardelle)
5 tablespoons unsalted butter
½ medium kabocha, cut into
    ¼-inch cubes (about 1½ cups)
1 shallot, finely chopped
    Salt and freshly ground black
    pepper
2 tablespoons chopped fresh
    thyme
    Freshly grated Parmesan cheese

If you've never had kabocha before, stop reading right now and go buy one. They keep for weeks on the counter, and their emerald green skin makes them a decorative addition to your fruit basket. The firm orange flesh is like a cross between butternut squash and sweet potato, making them perfect for both savory and sweet dishes. You can find kabocha in Asian markets or well-stocked supermarkets.

This pasta takes almost no time to prepare, and the nutty brown butter and sweet and creamy kabocha are a perfect accompaniment for each other. *Serves 4*

Prepare the pasta according to the package instructions.

While the pasta is cooking, melt the butter in a medium pan over medium-high heat. Add the kabocha and shallot and cook, stirring occasionally, until the kabocha is tender, about 10 minutes. Season to taste with salt and pepper.

Place the cooked pasta in a large bowl. Add the kabocha mixture and any butter in the pan and toss gently. Add the thyme, toss gently, and serve immediately with the cheese.

MAKE IT EASY
If you're having a hard time finding kabocha, you can use butternut squash instead.

SIX
Vegetarian

Spanish Tortilla *by Matt Armendariz,* **mattbites.com**

2 pounds russet potatoes, peeled
and cut into ¼-inch-thick slices

1 teaspoon sea salt or kosher salt

4 tablespoons extra-virgin olive
oil, divided

2 large onions, thinly sliced

6 large eggs
Salt and freshly ground black
pepper
Chopped fresh Italian parsley,
for garnish

This delicious, filling omelet is made with six basic, inexpensive ingredients. Once you try this, you'll want to add it to your regular dinner rotation. *Serves 4*

Preheat the oven to 400°F. Place the potatoes and salt in a large saucepan, add cold water to cover the potatoes, and bring to a boil over high heat. Reduce the heat to medium and simmer until the potatoes are tender, about 7 minutes. Drain the potatoes, rinse them with cold water, and drain again. Spread the potato slices on paper towels and pat dry.

Heat 2 tablespoons of the oil in a medium ovenproof skillet over medium heat. Add the onions and cook, stirring often, until golden-brown, about 5 minutes. Remove the onions from the heat and set aside.

In a large bowl, lightly beat the eggs. Add the cooked potato slices and onions, stir gently, and season generously with salt and pepper.

Heat the remaining 2 tablespoons oil in the same skillet over medium heat. Add the egg mixture and cook, undisturbed, until the bottom of the tortilla is lightly browned, about 2 minutes.

Transfer the skillet to the oven and bake until the eggs are set and the potatoes are very tender, about 20 minutes. Remove the tortilla from the oven and let it cool for 5 minutes. Loosen the tortilla from the pan by running the tip of a knife around the edge of the tortilla. Place a round platter over the pan and invert. Cut the tortilla into wedges, garnish with parsley, and serve.

Matt Armendariz, **mattbites.com**

Matt Armendariz is the graphic designer, art director, and food photographer behind the blog Matt Bites (mattbites.com). He's a man obsessed with food, drink, and everything in between. His site has been featured in various publications and he has appeared on television alongside Martha Stewart. His blog was selected as one of the world's Top 50 Food Blogs by the *London Times* online. He lives in Los Angeles with his partner, Adam Pearson, a food stylist, and their three incredibly small dogs.

More About Matt

What do you always have in your shopping cart?
A good olive oil, cheese, pasta, and peanut butter. Not all at the same time, of course.

What's your go-to weeknight dinner?
Omelets of any kind, or a very simple pasta dish.

What's your favorite kitchen tool?
A Microplane or zester. It's perfect for finishing a dish with cheese, as well as great for zesting citrus to bring that bright note to a dish.

Is there anything you just can't eat?
Nope. I will literally eat anything!

Black Bean, Quinoa, & Oat Burgers

by Kath Younger, **katheats.com**

3 small carrots, peeled and
 coarsely chopped

1 celery stalk, coarsely chopped

1½ cups cooked red quinoa

1 cup old-fashioned rolled oats

1 14-ounce can black beans,
 lightly drained

1 large egg

1 teaspoon dried oregano

⅛ teaspoon garlic powder or 1
 garlic clove, chopped

 Salt and freshly ground black
 pepper

8 hamburger buns

These burgers are a hearty and filling vegetarian dinner. They are made with pantry staples and ready in a flash, with minimal hands-on work. They hold together well, and baking them means there's no risk of their falling apart in a skillet.

Use this recipe as a blank slate for creative flavor possibilities—add curry powder and garam masala for a spicy twist, nuts for crunch, or lots of fresh herbs for flavor. You can serve these burgers with any fixings you like. This recipe makes eight burgers. *Serves 8*

Preheat the oven to 350°F. Place the carrots and celery in a food processor and pulse until minced. Add the quinoa, oats, beans, egg, oregano, and garlic. Season to taste with salt and pepper. Process until incorporated.

Form the black bean mixture into 8 patties. Place the patties on a greased baking sheet and bake until they are slightly firm, about 15 minutes. Turn over the burgers and bake until they are firm to the touch and begin to brown, 15 more minutes. Serve the burgers on the buns.

Farro with Carrots & Broccoli Rabe

by Rachel Rappaport, coconutandlime.com

Farro is an ancient grain that is said to be the mother of all wheat varieties. Look for it in the health food or international aisle of your supermarket. Farro's nutty flavor holds its own against the slightly bitter broccoli rabe and sweet carrots in this recipe. *Serves 4*

Place the water and farro in a medium saucepan over high heat and bring to a boil. Reduce the heat to medium-low and simmer until the farro is tender, stirring occasionally, about 25 minutes. Drain the farro and transfer to a large bowl.

While the farro is cooking, heat the oil in a large pan over medium-high heat. Add the onion, carrot, and garlic and cook, stirring, until the onion is translucent, about 5 minutes. Add the broccoli rabe and parsley and cook until they begin to wilt, about 3 minutes. Remove from the heat.

Add the vegetables to the farro and stir. Add the balsamic vinegar and lemon juice and stir to combine. Serve hot or at room temperature.

- 1 quart water
- 1 cup farro
- 2 tablespoons olive oil
- 1 small onion, chopped
- 1 carrot, diced
- 2 garlic cloves, minced
- ½ pound broccoli rabe, coarsely chopped
- ⅛ pound fresh Italian parsley, coarsely chopped
- 1½ tablespoons balsamic vinegar
- 2 tablespoons fresh lemon juice

Sweet Gingery Tofu
by Catherine McCord, **weelicious.com**

This dish is so easy because you probably have most of the ingredients on hand, you need only one dish to mix them all in, and it's inexpensive to make: less than three dollars for four servings! Serve the tofu with some edamame and brown rice and you have a protein, carb, and vegetable that make a perfectly balanced, Asian-inspired meal. *Serves 4*

Preheat the oven to 350°F. To drain the excess water from the tofu, wrap the tofu in a clean dish towel, place the wrapped tofu in a bowl, place another bowl or other weight on top, and let the tofu sit for about 10 minutes. While the tofu is draining, add the vinegar, soy sauce, honey, ginger, and sesame oil to an 11×7-inch baking dish, whisking to combine.

Remove the tofu from the dish towel, pat dry, and cut into ½-inch-thick slices. Add the tofu slices to the marinade, turning to coat. Let marinate 20 minutes (or, if making ahead, cover, refrigerate, and marinate overnight). Bake until the tofu is golden and the edges are golden-brown, 30 to 35 minutes. Garnish with sesame seeds, if desired, and serve with the hot cooked rice and steamed edamame.

1 **pound firm or extra-firm tofu, rinsed**
¼ **cup rice vinegar**
3 **tablespoons soy sauce**
2 **tablespoons honey**
2 **tablespoons minced fresh ginger**
2 **tablespoons toasted sesame oil**
 Sesame seeds, for garnish (optional)
 Hot cooked brown rice
 Steamed edamame

MAKE IT EASY
Make extra marinade and use it another night for baking fish or chicken. The marinade will keep for 3 to 4 weeks when stored in an airtight container in the fridge.

Vegetarian

205

Mexican Polenta Casserole *by Kath Younger,* **katheats.com**

3 cups frozen chopped bell peppers

1 cup frozen corn kernels

1 14-ounce can diced tomatoes, drained

1 cup cooked navy beans

1 tablespoon taco seasoning (such as Lawry's)

½ teaspoon ground cumin

½ teaspoon red pepper flakes

½ teaspoon dried oregano

½ teaspoon garlic powder

½ cup quick-cooking polenta

1 cup shredded Mexican four-cheese blend

Casseroles are really just a means to eat ooey, gooey melted cheese, and this recipe is all about the rich, cheesy topping. To balance all the cheesy goodness, I like to pair this casserole with sautéed greens or a salad. *Serves 4*

Preheat the oven to 350°F. Place the bell peppers, corn, tomatoes, beans, taco seasoning, cumin, red pepper flakes, oregano, and garlic in a large skillet over medium heat and cook, stirring to combine, for 5 to 7 minutes.

While the vegetable mixture cooks, prepare the polenta according to the package instructions.

Transfer the hot vegetable mixture to a 3-quart baking dish. Spoon the cooked polenta over the vegetables and top the polenta with the cheese. Bake until the cheese is completely melted and begins to brown, 15 to 20 minutes. Serve immediately.

No-Cook Mexican Scoop *by Kath Younger,* katheats.com

This recipe is great for nights when it's too hot to cook. Combine the ingredients in a bowl and scoop 'em up with some wholesome corn chips—no heat necessary. Go crazy with the condiments—sour cream, Jack cheese, jalapeños, hot sauce, lime juice, whatever you like! *Serves 4*

Add the beans, bell peppers, and tomatoes to a large bowl and toss to combine. Season to taste with salt and black pepper. To serve, divide the mixture among 4 bowls and top each bowl with avocado and salsa. Serve with corn chips.

2   14-ounce cans pinto beans, rinsed and drained

2   green bell peppers, stemmed, seeded, and chopped

6   plum tomatoes, chopped and drained

    Salt and freshly ground black pepper

1   avocado, peeled, pitted, and cubed

½   cup salsa

    Corn chips

Southwestern Grilled Cheese Sandwiches with Roasted Chiles *by Laura Levy,* laurasbestrecipes.com

1 **cup grated Monterey Jack cheese**

½ **cup grated Gruyère cheese**

½ **cup grated sharp white Cheddar cheese**

4 **tablespoons (½ stick) butter, softened**

8 **slices rustic sourdough bread**

4 **mild Anaheim chiles, roasted, peeled, seeded, and cut into wide slivers**

½ **cup (packed) baby spinach leaves, stems removed**

Try using canned fire-roasted chiles in this recipe—they don't have as much of that freshly roasted flavor, but they work just fine when you're too busy to roast the chiles yourself. I recommend tasting the chiles before adding them to the sandwiches to make sure you can handle the heat. *Serves 4*

Place the cheeses in a medium bowl and toss to combine. Spread the butter thickly on one side of each slice of sourdough bread.

Heat a large nonstick skillet over medium heat. Place 2 slices of buttered bread in the skillet, buttered side down. Quickly top the bread slices with a thin layer of the cheese mixture, several chile slivers, another thin layer of cheese, and a layer of spinach. Top each with a second slice of bread, buttered side up.

Cover and cook until the sandwiches are golden-brown and the cheese is melted, about 3 minutes per side. Repeat with the remaining ingredients. Slice each sandwich on the diagonal and serve immediately.

Laura Levy, laurasbestrecipes.com

Laura Levy's love of food and wine runs as deep as her Wine Country roots. Raised in the coastal hamlet of Mendocino on the northern California coast, Laura was taught at a young age to make every meal a little special by using fresh, seasonal, and local ingredients. She now lives with her family near Boulder, Colorado, where she is a popular food blogger (Laura's Best Recipes, laurasbestrecipes.com) and owner of the culinary marketing company Gourmet Media Group. She is also working on a cookbook that features the coastal flavors of Mendocino.

More About Laura

What do you always have in your shopping cart?
Chile peppers, chipotles, and seasonal veggies.

What's your go-to weeknight dinner?
Fajitas or grilled seafood.

What's your favorite kitchen tool?
My Vitamix blender.

Is there anything you just can't eat?
I don't eat food from fast-food chains.

Chilled Soba Noodles *by Jaden Hair,* steamykitchen.com

1 pound dry soba noodles
2 cups soba dipping sauce
1 bunch scallions, thinly sliced lengthwise
1 tablespoon finely grated fresh ginger
1 tablespoon wasabi paste
Sesame seeds, for garnish (optional)

Soba noodles are a popular Japanese pasta made from buckwheat, which contains protein, magnesium, and potassium. The noodles can be served chilled with dipping sauce, as they are here, or in a hot broth. This dish incorporates soba dipping sauce (known as *mentsuyu* in Japanese and found in Asian markets), fresh scallions, and fresh ginger, and it's fun to eat! *Serves 4*

Cook the noodles according to the package instructions. Drain the noodles in a colander and rinse with cold water. Chill the noodles in an ice bath until very cold and drain well.

Place the noodles on 4 plates or in 4 bowls. Garnish the noodles with sesame seeds, if desired. Divide the soba sauce into 4 shallow bowls or teacups. Serve the scallions, ginger, and wasabi paste alongside.

To eat this dish, add some scallion, ginger, and wasabi to the dipping sauce, to taste. Dip the noodles into the sauce and eat.

MAKE IT EASY
A few minutes before the noodles have finished cooking, place 2 cups ice by the sink for your ice bath. To chill the noodles quickly, use your hands to gently stir the ice into the noodles.

"How we work family weeknight meals is that the boys help prep the ingredients, I cook, and my husband cleans. Don't tell anyone, but I think I have the best deal ever."

—*Jaden Hair*

Asparagus "Linguine" with Mint Pesto

by Marc Matsumoto, norecipes.com

1 small bunch fresh mint, stems removed

2 small garlic cloves, peeled

1 teaspoon kosher salt

2 teaspoons fresh lemon juice

½ cup plus 2 tablespoons olive oil, divided

½ cup freshly grated pecorino or Parmesan cheese

Freshly ground black pepper

2 bunches asparagus (about 2 pounds), trimmed

If you're on a gluten-free or low-carb diet, chances are you don't each much pasta. But if you're anything like me, it's something you crave a lot, which is how I discovered that asparagus makes for a great noodle. It's tender, yet with just enough structure to hold onto pesto or a pomodoro sauce.

To make the noodles, you can use a sharp knife or mandoline to slice each asparagus spear into thin, flat noodles, but if you plan on making these frequently, I'd recommend getting a tool called a negi cutter. A negi cutter is a knife with five very sharp blades spaced about $\frac{1}{8}$ inch apart, making it easy to cut your favorite vegetables into thin noodles. *Serves 4*

Place the mint, garlic, kosher salt, lemon juice, and ½ cup of the oil in a food processor and process, using a rubber spatula to scrape down the sides of the bowl, until finely minced and combined. Transfer to a small bowl; add the cheese and pepper and stir to combine. Set the mint pesto aside.

Use a sharp knife or mandoline (or a negi cutter) to slice each asparagus spear into thin, flat noodles.

Heat the remaining 2 tablespoons oil in a large pan over medium-high heat until the oil shimmers. Working in batches, add the asparagus noodles and stir-fry until bright green, 1 to 2 minutes. Remove the noodles from the heat, add the mint pesto to taste, season to taste with pepper, and toss to coat. Serve immediately.

Store any remaining pesto in an airtight container in the refrigerator for up to 2 days.

MAKE IT EASY
Slice the asparagus up to 2 days ahead of time; wrap the slices in a damp paper towel and store them in the fridge until ready to cook.

Fiesta Flapjacks *by Kath Younger,* **katheats.com**

Pancakes aren't just for lazy Sunday mornings! For an easy dinner, try mixing your favorite pancake mix with all kinds of savory combinations: smoked salmon and goat cheese, tomato sauce and mozzarella, and the following vegetarian-friendly recipe that is reminiscent of pupusas, a savory Salvadoran dish. *Serves 4*

In a large bowl, prepare 4 servings of pancake batter according to the package instructions. Place the beans, bell peppers, and corn in a medium bowl and toss to combine. Transfer ½ cup of the vegetable mixture to the pancake batter and stir. Cook the pancakes according to the package instructions.

Meanwhile, spray a medium skillet with nonstick cooking spray. Add the remaining vegetable mixture and the cumin to the skillet and cook over medium heat, stirring, until the vegetables are tender, about 5 minutes. Season to taste with salt and black pepper.

To serve, place the pancakes on plates and top with the cooked vegetables, avocado, sour cream, and salsa. Serve immediately.

Pancake mix
- 1 cup black beans, rinsed and drained
- 1 red bell pepper, stemmed, seeded, and chopped
- 2 green bell peppers, stemmed, seeded, and chopped
- 1 cup frozen corn kernels, thawed
  Nonstick cooking spray
- 1 teaspoon ground cumin
  Salt and freshly ground black pepper
- 1 avocado, peeled, pitted, and chopped
- ¼ cup sour cream
- ½ cup salsa

Vegetarian

Green Bean & Mushroom Risotto
by Rachel Rappaport, **coconutandlime.com**

5 cups chicken or vegetable broth
1½ tablespoons olive oil
1 tablespoon butter
¾ cup chopped cremini
  mushrooms
2 large shallots, finely chopped
2 garlic cloves, minced
  Salt and freshly ground black
  pepper
2 cups uncooked arborio rice
2 cups diced trimmed green beans
⅓ cup freshly grated Parmesan
  cheese

Many people think that risotto requires a lot of work, but that couldn't be further from the truth. Adding vegetables to this risotto recipe makes it a hearty, complete meal. What's more, the whole dish is ready to serve in about 20 minutes. Try this recipe when green beans are in season for the best result. *Serves 4*

Place the broth in a medium pot and bring to a simmer.

While the broth comes to a simmer, heat the oil and butter in a large saucepan over medium heat. Add the mushrooms, shallots, and garlic, season to taste with salt and pepper, and cook, stirring, until softened and golden-brown, 3 to 5 minutes. Add the rice to the saucepan and cook, stirring, for 2 minutes.

Add ½ cup of the hot broth to the saucepan and simmer, stirring often, until the broth is absorbed by the rice. Add more broth, ½ cup at a time, stirring often and allowing each addition to be absorbed before adding the next.

When about half of the broth has been added, add the green beans to the rice. Continue to cook, adding the remaining broth ½ cup at a time and stirring, until the rice is tender and the mixture is creamy. Remove from the heat, add the cheese, stir, and serve.

MAKE IT EASY
Use thin French green beans, which do not need to have their strings removed.

Spring Frittata *by Kath Younger,* katheats.com

Nonstick cooking spray
1 cup trimmed chopped asparagus (cut into 2-inch pieces)
¼ pound goat cheese, crumbled
1 cup sliced cherry tomatoes
1½ teaspoons dried oregano
   Kosher salt and freshly ground black pepper
8 large eggs
½ cup shredded Italian cheese blend

This frittata makes a light and bright dinner. Creamy, tangy pockets of goat cheese are the stars of this dish, but feel free to get creative with whatever cheeses you have on hand. Serve with sautéed greens or a side salad dressed simply with a little extra-virgin olive oil, salt, and a drizzle of honey. *Serves 4*

Preheat the broiler. Spray a large ovenproof skillet with nonstick cooking spray. Add the asparagus to the skillet and cook over medium-high heat, stirring occasionally, until tender, about 5 minutes. Add the goat cheese, tomatoes, oregano, and kosher salt and pepper to taste and stir to combine.

Beat the eggs in a medium bowl and add them to the skillet. Cook, undisturbed, until the eggs are just set on the edges, 2 to 3 minutes. Top with the Italian cheese. Transfer the skillet to the broiler and broil until the cheese begins to brown, about 5 minutes. Cut the frittata into wedges and serve immediately.

Tofu & Vegetable Fried Rice
by Andrea Meyers, andreasrecipes.com

Using leftovers is a great way to make fast meals. Whenever I cook rice, I like to make some extra and use it throughout the week in other dishes, such as this fried rice with tofu and fresh vegetables. Fried rice is very versatile—you can use many different kinds of vegetables in it, making it a perfect dish to help clean out the vegetable bin. *Serves 4*

Place the tofu and soy sauce in a medium bowl and toss gently. Marinate for about 5 minutes.

Heat 2 tablespoons of the oil in a wok or large skillet over medium-high heat. Add the tofu and cook, stirring, for 2 minutes. Add the carrots and bell pepper and cook, stirring, until the vegetables are crisp-tender, 2 to 3 minutes. Remove the vegetables and tofu and set aside.

Add the remaining 2 tablespoons oil to the hot pan and swirl to coat. Add the cooked rice and oyster sauce and cook, stirring to break up any clumps in the rice, until hot, about 3 minutes. Return the vegetables and tofu to the pan, stir, and cook for 1 to 2 more minutes. Serve immediately.

½ pound extra-firm tofu, drained, patted dry, and cut into ½-inch cubes

2 tablespoons low-sodium soy sauce

4 tablespoons canola oil, divided

2 medium carrots, peeled and thinly sliced on the diagonal

1 red bell pepper, stemmed, seeded, and chopped

4 cups leftover cooked brown or white rice

¼ cup oyster sauce

Chalupas *by Lori Lange,* recipegirl.com

Nonstick cooking spray

8 6-inch flour tortillas

2 cups refried beans, divided

2 cups shredded Monterey Jack and Cheddar cheese blend, divided

2 cups finely chopped lettuce

1 cup salsa

1 cup sour cream

1 cup guacamole (optional)

My mother had this very simple meal in the weekly dinner rotation when I was growing up. With a bunch of hungry kids to feed, my mother could whip this up quickly when she got home from work, and the ingredients were affordable. It's now a favorite in my own family. *Serves 4*

Preheat the oven to 400°F. Spray a baking sheet with nonstick cooking spray. Place 4 tortillas on the baking sheet and heat on the center rack in the oven for 4 minutes.

Remove the baking sheet from the oven and turn over the tortillas. Spread each tortilla with ¼ cup of the refried beans and top with ¼ cup of the cheese. Bake until the cheese is hot and bubbling and the tortillas are crisp, 5 to 7 minutes. Repeat with the remaining tortillas. Serve immediately, topping each tortilla with lettuce, salsa, sour cream, and guacamole, if desired.

Black Bean Burritos with Feta

by Julie Van Rosendaal, **dinnerwithjulie.com**

Black beans are inexpensive, convenient, and nutritionally stellar—they're packed with fiber, protein, vitamins, and minerals and are low in fat and calories. If you can doctor them up, a can of beans is the ultimate fast food. If you don't feel like making these vegetarian and want to give these burritos a boost, cook a crumbled chorizo sausage along with the onion until no longer pink. You can also substitute pinto beans for the black beans, if you prefer.

If you like, wrap the tortillas in foil and warm them in a 300°F oven while you make the filling. *Serves 4*

Heat the oil in a large skillet over medium-high heat. Add the onion and cook, stirring, until softened, about 5 minutes. Add the bell pepper, jalapeño, and garlic and cook, stirring, until the peppers are softened, about 5 more minutes. Add the beans, salsa, and cumin and cook, lightly mashing some of the beans with the back of a spoon, until the mixture is hot and begins to thicken, about 5 more minutes. Add the cheese, stir, and remove the skillet from the heat.

Spoon the filling down the middle of each tortilla and add cilantro, if desired. Fold one long side of each tortilla over the filling to cover; fold up the short ends, then roll up the burrito. Serve the burritos warm, with sour cream and salsa.

1 tablespoon olive or canola oil
1 small onion, finely chopped
1 small red bell pepper, stemmed, seeded, and finely chopped
1 jalapeño chile, seeded and finely chopped
2 garlic cloves, crushed
1 19-ounce can black beans, rinsed and drained
½ cup salsa, plus additional for serving
½ teaspoon ground cumin
½ cup crumbled feta cheese
4 10-inch flour tortillas
¼ cup chopped fresh cilantro leaves (optional)
Sour cream

Kate Jones, **ourbestbites.com**

Kate Randle Jones was born and raised in Logan, Utah. After graduating from high school, she broke her father's heart and attended his ultimate rival school, Brigham Young University, where she earned a degree in English. Although she always loved experimenting with food, she didn't really start cooking until she discovered that two newlyweds who are also college students generally live right around the poverty line. She found that she enjoyed cooking from scratch with fresh ingredients and learned to express love and creativity through food that nearly anyone could make and enjoy. In 2008, she and her good friend Sara Wells established Our Best Bites (ourbestbites.com), a cooking blog that focuses on fresh, high-quality food that's fun to make and eat. She and her husband, Sam, recently purchased an old Southern home with a big yard in Louisiana, where they live with their young son and daughter and their cat.

More About Kate

What do you always have in your shopping cart?
Limes, garlic, cilantro, one or two kids, and a Diet Coke to keep me sane.

What's your go-to weeknight dinner?
Spinach and feta pasta, from our blog. It's super-fast, easy, delicious, and good for you!

What's your favorite kitchen tool?
Definitely a toss-up between my pizza cutter and my cookie scoop, just because they're both so versatile.

Is there anything you just can't eat?
Okra. I truly believe it's a vegetable straight from hell, hoed by the devil himself.

Chorizo & Kidney Bean Chowder

by Julie Van Rosendaal, **dinnerwithjulie.com**

This hearty soup is a great way to feed the whole family with a single sausage, because it uses the meat as a seasoning to flavor the entire pot. If you like, serve it over a scoop of hot cooked rice to complete the protein in the beans. *Serves 4*

Heat the oil in a large pot over medium heat. Add the chorizo, onion, celery, and jalapeño and cook, breaking up the sausage with a spoon, until the onion is softened and the meat is no longer pink, about 5 minutes.

Add the potato, broth, corn, beans, salsa, water, and cumin and bring to a simmer. Reduce the heat to low and cook, stirring occasionally, until the potatoes are tender and the soup has thickened, about 30 minutes. Season to taste with salt and pepper. Serve hot.

1 tablespoon canola or olive oil
1 fresh chorizo sausage, casing removed
1 small onion, chopped
1 small celery stalk, chopped
1 jalapeño chile, seeded and minced
1 thin-skinned potato (such as Yukon Gold), diced
1 quart chicken or vegetable broth
1 16-ounce can kernel corn, drained
1 14-ounce can kidney beans, rinsed and drained
1 cup salsa
1 cup water
1 teaspoon ground cumin
   Salt and freshly ground black pepper

MAKE IT EASY

This is a great soup to make ahead, stash in the fridge, and dip into all week long; its flavor actually improves after a day or two. Store it covered in the fridge and it will keep for 1 week.

Soups & Stews

245

Warm & Hearty Taco Soup *by Jenny Flake,* **picky-palate.com**

- 2 tablespoons extra-virgin olive oil
- 1 medium onion, finely chopped
- 1 green bell pepper, stemmed, seeded, and chopped
- 4 garlic cloves, minced
- 1 pound lean ground beef
- ½ teaspoon salt
- ¼ teaspoon freshly ground black pepper
- 2 14-ounce cans chicken broth
- 1 pound frozen corn kernels
- 1 14-ounce can black beans, rinsed and drained
- 1 14-ounce can kidney beans, rinsed and drained
- 1 14-ounce can great northern beans, rinsed and drained
- 1 10-ounce can diced tomatoes
- 1 10-ounce can plus one 4-ounce can diced mild green chiles
- 1 1-ounce package dry ranch dressing mix
- 2 tablespoons taco seasoning (such as Lawry's)
  Sour cream, for garnish
  Corn chips or tortilla chips, for garnish
  Fresh cilantro leaves, for garnish

Get creative with this soup by garnishing it with your favorite taco toppings, like sour cream and cilantro. This recipe suggest corn chips as a garnish; salsa and scallions are other options.

Serve half and save half: this soup can be frozen in an airtight container for up to a month. *Serves 8*

Heat the oil in a large pot over medium heat. Add the onion and bell pepper and cook, stirring, until softened, about 5 minutes. Add the garlic and cook, stirring, for 1 minute. Add the ground beef, salt, and black pepper and cook, breaking up the meat with a spatula, until the beef is browned, 5 to 7 minutes. Add the chicken broth, corn, beans, tomatoes, chiles, ranch dressing mix, and taco seasoning; stir to combine. Reduce the heat to low and simmer until hot, about 15 minutes.

Pour the soup into 8 bowls. Garnish with sour cream, corn or tortilla chips, and cilantro and serve.

EIGHT

Side Dishes

Spicy Bean-Stuffed Bell Peppers
by Kath Younger, katheats.com

- 2 cups water
- ½ cup coarse or medium bulgur
- 1 teaspoon kosher salt
- ¾ cup cooked pinto beans
- ¾ cup cooked navy beans
- 1 14-ounce can diced tomatoes, drained
- 2 tablespoons diced pickled jalapeño chiles
- ½ tablespoon dried oregano
- 1 teaspoon hot sauce, or to taste
- ¼ teaspoon ground cumin
- ¼ teaspoon freshly ground black pepper
- 4 bell peppers, stemmed, seeded, and halved
- 4 slices Muenster cheese, cut in half

This recipe is great if you have leftover beans and grains to use up and need to morph them into a quick weeknight side; the pepper halves make perfect single-serving bowls. Go crazy with beans and grains in this recipe—use whatever you have on hand or mix up a few different kinds. I used bulgur here, but you can swap in brown rice, millet, or quinoa—whatever you fancy!

For a healthy vegetarian main course, just double the recipe. You can find bulgur, also called cracked wheat, in supermarkets or natural food stores. *Serves 4*

Bring the water to a boil in a medium saucepan; add the bulgur and kosher salt and remove from the heat. Cover and let stand until the bulgur is tender, about 30 minutes. Drain well and transfer to a large bowl.

Preheat the oven to 400°F. Add the beans, tomatoes, jalapeños, oregano, hot sauce, cumin, and black pepper to the bulgur and mix well. Divide the bulgur mixture among the bell pepper halves and bake until the filling is hot and the peppers are tender, about 20 minutes. Top each pepper half with 1 slice of cheese and bake until the cheese is melted, about 5 more minutes. Serve immediately.

MAKE IT EASY
Use canned beans instead of cooking your own and you won't have to do any planning ahead.

Broccoli Crunch Salad *by Matt Armendariz,* **mattbites.com**

1 cup mayonnaise
¼ cup honey
¼ cup apple cider vinegar
4 cups chopped broccoli florets
2 scallions, diced
½ cup chopped red onion
⅓ cup walnuts
⅓ cup golden raisins
2 tablespoons sunflower seeds

You'll find versions of this salad all over the place. Some call for a quick blanching of the broccoli, and others cook it until it's mush. Why bother, when raw broccoli is so crunchy and good?

Note that a salad like this is adaptable; add more or less of anything you like. *Serves 4*

Place the mayonnaise, honey, and vinegar in a small bowl and whisk to combine; set the dressing aside.

Place the remaining ingredients in a large bowl and toss to combine. Add the dressing, toss to coat, and refrigerate, covered, for up to 2 hours. Serve immediately.

Sautéed Chickpeas & Spinach

by Shauna James Ahern and Daniel Ahern, **glutenfreegirl.com**

This is the fastest meal we know. If Shauna is in a rush, or she wants to make a quick lunch for herself and our toddler, she heats up a pan and starts cooking this. It's always good.

You should feel free to experiment with different spices to jazz up the flavor. We love smoked paprika or cumin, which you would add just after the garlic. We also like to add a little sliced prosciutto or Serrano ham, or broccoli spears, just after the chickpeas. For a final touch, top with an egg that has been soft-poached or fried with frizzled edges. *Serves 4*

Heat the oil in a large sauté pan over medium-high heat. Add the garlic and cook, stirring, until it begins to brown, about 1 minute.

Add the chickpeas and cook, stirring, until they are hot and begin to brown, about 3 minutes. Add the spinach and cook, stirring, until it is wilted, about 2 minutes. Add the lemon juice and season to taste with salt and pepper. Serve immediately.

2 tablespoons olive oil
2 garlic cloves, thinly sliced
2 14-ounce cans chickpeas, rinsed and drained
1 large bunch spinach, stems removed
2 tablespoons fresh lemon juice
   Salt and freshly ground black pepper

Vegetarian

Cheese Tacos *by Elise Bauer*, simplyrecipes.com

1   tablespoon butter
8   6-inch corn tortillas
2   cups shredded Cheddar or Monterey Jack cheese
1   small apple, cored and thinly sliced
½   avocado, peeled, pitted, and cut into 8 slices
1   cup shredded lettuce
1½ cups salsa

Usually cheese tacos just have cheese in them. Add some salsa and you're done. My cheese tacos tend to be a little more elaborate. I stand by my rule that you can put almost anything in a tortilla and call it a taco. I'm the only one in the family who puts slices of apples in my tacos, however, prompting turned-up noses from everyone else. Like I said, you can put anything you want in a tortilla and call it a taco, and I like apples and avocados in my cheese tacos.

This is a very simple, versatile, and tasty dinner that can be as varied as the ingredients you have on hand. You'll just need corn tortillas, some cheese, and whatever additional fillings you like; you can also add leftover beef, chicken, or pork. *Serves 4*

Heat a large cast-iron pan over medium-high heat. Spread a small amount of the butter on one side of 1 tortilla. When the pan is hot (it should sizzle when sprinkled with a few drops of water), place the tortilla in the pan, buttered side down. Using a spatula, flip the tortilla several times until both sides are covered in melted butter, then let the tortilla cook until pockets of air begin forming bubbles in the tortilla, about 3 minutes.

Add about ¼ cup of the cheese to half the tortilla and, using the spatula, fold over the other side of the tortilla. Move the folded cheese taco to one side of the pan. Lightly butter a second tortilla, add it to the pan, and repeat the process. Cook each cheese taco until the cheese is melted, about 4 minutes per taco, then remove from the pan. Repeat with the remaining tortillas and cheese.

Open each taco and add 1 or 2 apple slices, 1 avocado slice, and the desired amount of lettuce. Arrange on plates and serve with the salsa.

MAKE IT EASY
Make this recipe even easier by using the microwave. First, soften the tortillas: place the tortillas on a paper towel to absorb moisture and heat them in the microwave for 20 seconds per tortilla. Once they've been softened, add the cheese, fold them over, and heat them for a few more seconds, just until the cheese melts. Then add the fillings and dinner is served!

SEVEN

Soups & Stews

Pork Belly, Kimchi, & Tofu Stew

by Matt Armendariz, **mattbites.com**

2 tablespoons extra-virgin olive oil

2 cups kimchi, undrained

⅔ pound pork belly, thinly sliced

1 tablespoon garlic, minced

1½ cups water

2 tablespoons Korean chili paste (gochujang)

1 tablespoon low-sodium soy sauce

½ pound medium-firm tofu, cut into 1-inch cubes

Hot cooked rice

1 scallion, thinly sliced

1 tablespoon Korean dried chili flakes (gochugaru; optional)

This soup, with its roots in Korean cuisine, is packed with flavor and wonderful on chilly nights. Pork belly is uncured bacon and comes from the same cut; ask your butcher for some if it's not readily available. Find kimchi, Korean chili paste, and Korean dried chili flakes in Asian markets. *Serves 4*

Heat the oil in a medium pot over medium-high heat. Add the kimchi, with its juices, and stir. Add the pork belly and garlic and stir to combine. Cook the mixture for about 5 minutes. Add the water, chili paste, and soy sauce and stir gently to combine. Bring the mixture to a boil.

When the stew begins to boil, add the tofu, cover, and reduce the heat to medium-low. Let the stew simmer for about 25 minutes. Serve the stew over the hot cooked rice, topped with the scallion and chili flakes.

Tuscan White Bean & Chicken Soup

by Jenny Flake, **picky-palate.com**

This no-fuss dinner will amaze you with how fast it is to put together. Make sure to shred your rotisserie chicken ahead of time and save any extras for another quick dinner. Use your family's favorite pasta sauce and enjoy! *Serves 4*

Place the soup, chicken broth, and marinara sauce in a medium saucepan over medium heat and cook, stirring, until hot, about 5 minutes. Add the chicken and beans, reduce the heat to low, and simmer until the chicken and beans are hot, about 10 minutes. Serve immediately.

- 2 10.75-ounce cans cream of chicken soup
- 1½ cups chicken broth
- 1 cup marinara sauce
- 2 cups shredded rotisserie chicken
- 1 14-ounce can great northern beans, rinsed and drained

Southern Chicken & Dumplings

by Christy Jordan, **southernplate.com**

1 10.75-ounce can cream of
   chicken soup
2 14-ounce cans chicken broth
½ cup all-purpose flour
¼ teaspoon salt
¼ teaspoon freshly ground black
   pepper
1 10-count can flaky biscuits
1 rotisserie chicken, skin
   discarded, deboned, shredded
   Fresh Italian parsley, for garnish

Chicken and dumplings is a staple where I'm from, a dish steeped in the tradition of harder times and large families. It was developed as a means of stretching a meal to feed as many people as possible, and this is the recipe my mother and grandmother always used. Whenever anyone found out this was for supper at our house, we always had guests show up to get a bite! You'll want to avoid stirring these dumplings as they cook; simply use a spatula to push them down into the broth from time to time. *Serves 4 to 6*

Place the soup and chicken broth in a medium pot over medium-high heat and bring to a gentle boil.

While the soup and broth are coming to a boil, place the flour, salt, and pepper in a small bowl and stir to combine. Separate each biscuit into 3 layers. Dip both sides of each biscuit layer in the flour mixture. Tear each dipped biscuit layer into 3 pieces and place them in the gently boiling broth.

Reduce the heat to medium, add the shredded chicken to the pot, and continue cooking until the dumplings are firm, about 10 minutes. Serve immediately, garnished with parsley.

©2010 Jennifer Davick

Shauna James Ahern and Daniel Ahern, **glutenfreegirl.com**

Shauna James Ahern writes the popular website Gluten-Free Girl and the Chef (glutenfreegirl.com), which was named one of the best food sites in the world by Gourmet.com, Bon Appetit.com, and the *London Times*, as well as being named one of the 20 best blogs by and for women by the *Sunday Telegraph*. Gluten-Free Girl and the Chef was named Best Food Blog with a Theme in the 2005 Food Blog Awards, and it receives thousands of hits a day. Shauna's first book, *Gluten-Free Girl: How I Found the Food That Loves Me Back and How You Can Too* (Wiley) is now available in paperback. Her first cookbook, *Gluten-Free Girl and the Chef: A Love Story in 100 Tempting Recipes* (Wiley), written with her husband, Daniel, was published in the fall of 2010.

Daniel Ahern has chef experience at a variety of restaurants from coast to coast, from Gramercy Tavern in New York to Papillon in Denver. When he was the executive chef at Impromptu Wine Bar in Seattle, he received national recognition for turning the restaurant gluten-free. He now cooks at The Hardware Store on Vashon Island in Washington, where he lives with Shauna and their daughter.

More About Daniel and Shauna

What do you always have in your shopping cart?
Olive oil, eggs, lemons, butter, garlic, onions, bacon, quinoa, yogurt, and cheese.

What's your go-to weeknight dinner?
Roasted lemon chicken with jasmine rice, pan gravy, and roasted broccoli.

What's your favorite kitchen tool?
The coffeemaker, for the morning. Good knives all day. The juicer, to add flavor.

Is there anything you just can't eat?
American cheese for Danny. Gluten for Shauna.

Slow-Cooker Beef Bourguignon

by Shauna James Ahern and Daniel Ahern, **glutenfreegirl.com**

This is a great comfort food in the fall and winter. The tender beef melts in your mouth, and the carrots, mushrooms, and onions build a depth of flavor that mingles with the red wine. Serve this over rice, potatoes, or pasta, or on its own as a stew. You can't go wrong. If you're cooking this gluten-free, use sorghum flour or sweet rice flour instead of regular flour. *Serves 6 to 8*

Cook the bacon pieces in a large skillet over medium-high heat until crisp and browned. Transfer the bacon to paper towels to drain, reserving the bacon fat in the skillet. When drained, transfer the bacon to the refrigerator.

Season the beef generously with salt and pepper. Add the beef to the skillet and cook over medium-high heat until browned, 3 to 4 minutes. Add the flour and stir to coat evenly. Remove from the heat, add the cognac, and stir. Return the skillet to medium-high heat and add the broth and tomato paste, stirring and scraping the browned bits from the bottom of the pan. Bring the mixture to a boil and remove from the heat. Transfer the beef mixture to a slow cooker and add the wine, bay leaf, and garlic.

Add the oil to the skillet and heat over medium-high heat. Add the pearl onions and cook, stirring, until they begin to caramelize, about 5 minutes. Add the mushrooms and carrot and cook, stirring, until they begin to brown, 7 to 8 minutes. Add the thyme and cook until fragrant, about 1 minute. Transfer the vegetables to the slow cooker and stir to combine.

Cover and cook on low for 8 to 10 hours, or on high for 5 to 6 hours. Remove the bay leaf before serving.

6 slices bacon, cut into
  1- to 2-inch pieces
1 3-pound beef rump roast,
  trimmed and cut into 1-inch
  cubes
  Salt and freshly ground black
  pepper
3 tablespoons all-purpose flour
⅓ cup cognac
1½ cups chicken or beef broth
1 tablespoon tomato paste
1 cup Burgundy or other red wine
1 whole bay leaf
2 garlic cloves, minced
1 tablespoon olive oil
½ pound pearl onions, peeled
1 pound button mushrooms,
  sliced
1 large carrot, peeled and sliced
2 tablespoons chopped fresh
  thyme

Slow-Cooker Jambalaya *by Jaden Hair,* steamykitchen.com

This chicken, sausage, and shrimp jambalaya is one of my family's favorites. When it's cooked "low and slow" in the slow cooker, the chicken is especially tender and delicious.

You'll want to prep and get this recipe going in the morning—the jambalaya needs four to six hours of cooking time on the slow cooker's high setting, or six to eight hours if cooked on low. *Serves 4 to 6*

Heat the oil in a large sauté pan over medium-high heat. Add the chicken and sausage, season to taste with salt and black pepper, and cook, turning once, until browned, about 8 minutes. Transfer the chicken and sausage to a slow cooker, reserving the oil in the pan.

Add the celery, bell pepper, onion, and garlic to the pan and cook over medium-high heat, stirring, until the vegetables are softened and fragrant, about 2 minutes.

Transfer the vegetables to the slow cooker. Add the broth, crushed tomatoes, Cajun seasoning, paprika, 1 teaspoon salt, 1 teaspoon black pepper, and Tabasco sauce. Cover and cook on low for 6 to 8 hours, or on high for 4 to 6 hours.

Once the jambalaya is cooked, turn off the slow cooker and skim away any excess oil on the surface. Add the shrimp and stir until pink, 3 to 5 minutes. (The residual heat from the slow cooker will suffice to cook the shrimp.) If desired, add more salt, black pepper, and Tabasco sauce. Serve the jambalaya over hot cooked rice or with bread.

2 tablespoons olive oil

1 pound boneless skinless chicken thighs, cut into 1-inch pieces

1 pound smoked sausage, cut into 1-inch-thick pieces

1 teaspoon kosher or sea salt, plus additional for seasoning

1 teaspoon freshly ground black pepper, plus additional for seasoning

2 celery stalks, diced

1 bell pepper, stemmed, seeded, and diced

1 small onion, diced

2 garlic cloves, minced

1 quart chicken or vegetable broth

1 14.5-ounce can crushed tomatoes

2 teaspoons Cajun seasoning

1 teaspoon smoked paprika

½ teaspoon Tabasco or hot sauce, or to taste

½ pound shrimp, peeled and deveined

3 cups hot cooked rice or 1 large baguette

MAKE IT EASY
Dice the celery, bell pepper, and onion the night before to save on prep time in the morning.

"Throw everything in the pot, plug it in, and push a button. Don't you wish everything in life were this easy?!"

–Jaden Hair

Healthy Slow-Cooker Beef Chili
by Catherine McCord, weelicious.com

1 tablespoon olive oil
1 pound lean ground beef
1 small onion, diced
2 celery stalks, diced
1 red bell pepper, stemmed,
   seeded, and diced
2 garlic cloves, minced
1 28-ounce can tomato sauce
1 28-ounce can diced tomatoes
2 14-ounce cans kidney beans,
   rinsed and drained or 2 cups
   cooked kidney beans
1 tablespoon salt
1 tablespoon ground cumin
2 tablespoons chili powder

This is the perfect recipe to make when you wake up and want to toss everything in a slow cooker and come home eight to ten hours later to a home-cooked meal. The best part is that this chili freezes beautifully, so you have to cook only once for two nights of dinner for four! *Serves 8*

Heat the oil in a large sauté pan over medium-high heat until the oil shimmers. Add the ground beef and cook, breaking up the meat with a spatula, until browned and fully cooked, about 5 minutes. Drain the grease and transfer the cooked beef to a slow cooker. Add the remaining ingredients to the slow cooker and stir to combine. Cover and cook on low for 8 to 10 hours. Serve hot.

The chili can be refrigerated for up to 5 days, or frozen in an airtight container for up to 4 months.

MAKE IT EASY
Dice the vegetables the night before so everything can be tossed in the slow cooker the next morning. If you want to make this chili with an extra kick, just add an additional tablespoon of chili powder.

Catherine McCord, **weelicious.com**

Catherine McCord is a model, actress, and mother of two. She launched Weelicious (weelicious.com) in 2007, providing a solution to parents' hectic lives by showing them how to cook recipes that are kid-friendly, quick, and nutritious. With a background at New York City's prestigious Institute of Culinary Education and a passion for food, Catherine has developed recipes that appeal to a range of ages—from infants starting on solid foods, to school kids and adults. Weelicious focuses on educating kids and involving them in the process with how-to cooking videos featuring her three-year-old son, Kenya, and one-year old daughter, Chloe. With a new recipe or tip debuting daily, Weelicious is a wealth of information for parents and a visual delight for foodies of any age.

More About Catherine

What do you always have in your shopping cart?

We generally buy 80 percent of our food at our local farmers' market. In that cart I've always got eggs, whole chickens, fruits, veggies, honey, sourdough bread, sweet potatoes, Cheddar cheese, organic decaf coffee, lettuce, and salmon. When I shop at the supermarket, it's usually for things like mustard or soy sauce, milk, yogurt, oatmeal, and cereal.

What's your go-to weeknight dinner?

I make a whole chicken in a slow cooker at least once a week. It gives me dinner that night and leftover meat for quesadillas; tacos; or mac, chicken, and cheese bites for lunch or dinner the next day.

What's your favorite kitchen tool?

My Kyocera hand mandoline. I use it to shave veggies into salads, make potato chips, and more!

Is there anything you just can't eat?

Lamb! I've tried so many times, even when I was on vacation in Chile, where it's as fresh and tasty as you'll ever find it. Just can't do it!

Wild Mushroom Soup *by Kath Younger,* **katheats.com**

2 teaspoons olive oil

2 pounds assorted fresh
   mushrooms, chopped

2 large carrots, peeled and
   chopped

2 large celery stalks, chopped

3 garlic cloves, minced

2 14-ounce cans low-sodium beef
   broth

2 10.5-ounce cans low-sodium
   cream of mushroom soup

1 cup cooked navy beans
   Chopped walnuts, for garnish

This recipe looks fancy, but it is so easy to make! The hardest part is foraging for wild mushrooms—or you can just pick up a few varieties at the grocery store. Be bold and move beyond the button mushroom—try cremini, oyster, or even enoki mushrooms for rich and varied earthy flavors. You can use drained canned navy beans instead of cooking them from scratch. *Serves 4*

Heat the oil in a large pot over medium heat. Add the mushrooms, carrots, celery, and garlic and cook, stirring, until tender, about 7 minutes. Add the beef broth, soup, and beans, stir, reduce the heat to low, and simmer until the soup is fragrant and thick, 10 to 15 minutes.

Remove the pot from the heat and use an immersion blender to puree the soup, leaving some chunks intact (or cool the soup slightly and puree three-fourths of the soup in a standing blender or food processor before returning it to the pot). Serve immediately, garnished with walnuts.

Ten-Minute Miso Soup *by Jaden Hair,* steamykitchen.com

This quick soup is worth a trip to the Asian market (or the Asian foods aisle of your supermarket) to pick up ingredients that you might not have on hand already: miso, dashi, and wakame. Miso is a fermented soybean paste that's a staple of Japanese cooking; I prefer using shiro miso in this recipe because it's light and not too salty. Dashi is a fish-based soup stock, and its instant variety, used here, is called dashi-no-moto. And wakame is a type of seaweed commonly used in soups and salads—it looks a bit like tea leaves when it's dried, and it unfurls into beautiful green strips when soaked in water.

Be sure to add the miso to the broth only after you've removed it from the heat—this prevents it from getting too grainy or gritty. *Serves 4*

- 1 tablespoon dried wakame
- 1 quart water
- 1½ teaspoons instant dashi granules
- ½ cup cubed medium tofu
- ½ cup shiro miso
- 2 tablespoons chopped scallions, for garnish

Place the wakame in a small bowl of warm water. Boil 1 quart water in a large pot over medium-high heat. Add the instant dashi to the pot, whisking to dissolve. Reduce the heat to medium-low and add the tofu. Drain the wakame and add it to the pot. Simmer for 2 minutes.

While the dashi broth simmers, spoon the miso into a bowl. Ladle about ½ cup of the hot dashi broth into the bowl and whisk, combining it with the miso to make a smooth mixture.

Remove the pot from the heat, add the miso mixture to the pot, and stir well. Serve immediately, garnished with scallions.

MAKE IT EASY

To save yourself trips to the market, you can keep miso paste in an airtight container in the fridge for about 6 months, and you can keep instant dashi and wakame in your pantry for a very long time. To make this soup heartier, try adding vegetables like carrots and snow peas.

Italian Sausage Soup *by Kate Jones,* **ourbestbites.com**

1 tablespoon olive oil

½ pound Italian turkey sausage

1 small onion, minced

5 garlic cloves, minced

1 32-ounce box chicken broth

1 14.5-ounce can diced tomatoes with Italian herbs, undrained

1 teaspoon dried basil

1 teaspoon dried oregano

¼ cup chopped fresh Italian parsley

½ teaspoon dried marjoram

1 14-ounce can chickpeas, rinsed and drained

6 cups (loosely packed) spinach leaves

Freshly grated Parmesan cheese (optional)

This recipe makes a lot, but it's even tastier the next day. Try reheating a bowl of this soup for a quick and healthy lunch the next day, or serve it as leftovers that no one will complain about. *Serves 6 to 8*

Heat the oil in a large pot over medium-high heat. Add the sausage and cook, stirring, until it begins to brown, 4 to 5 minutes. Add the onion and garlic and cook, stirring, until the onion is translucent and the garlic is fragrant, 2 to 3 minutes.

Add the chicken broth, tomatoes, basil, oregano, parsley, marjoram, and chickpeas. Reduce the heat to medium, stir, cover, and simmer for 10 to 15 minutes. Stir in the spinach and cook until it is wilted, 3 to 5 minutes. Serve with the cheese, if desired.

MAKE IT EASY

If you're having a hard time finding Italian turkey sausage, you can substitute ½ pound lean ground turkey and 2 teaspoons Italian sausage seasoning, which you can usually find in the spice section of the supermarket.

Yuca with Yogurt Mojo *by Marc Matsumoto,* norecipes.com

Yuca, also called cassava, is packed with nutrients such as calcium, phosphorus, and vitamin C. It's poisonous and often bitter when uncooked, so it's important you cook it completely.

Dressed with olive oil and a tangy yogurt mojo sauce, yuca makes the perfect side dish for grilled meats and seafood. *Serves 4*

Place the yogurt, garlic, lemon juice, and kosher salt in a medium bowl and stir to combine. Set the yogurt mojo aside.

Place the yuca in a large pot of salted water and bring to a boil. Reduce the heat to low and simmer until the yuca is pierced easily with a fork, 15 to 20 minutes. Drain the yuca and transfer it to another medium bowl. Add the oil, tossing gently to coat.

Transfer the yuca to a plate and pour the yogurt mojo over it. Top with the cilantro and pepper. Serve immediately.

½ cup plain yogurt
2 garlic cloves, minced
1 tablespoon fresh lemon juice
½ teaspoon kosher salt
2 small yuca roots, peeled and cut into 1-inch chunks
¼ cup olive oil
　Fresh cilantro leaves
　Freshly ground black pepper

Grilled Zucchini with Feta, Olives, & Thyme

by Matt Armendariz, **mattbites.com**

- 4 **large zucchini, trimmed and thinly sliced lengthwise**
- ¼ **cup extra-virgin olive oil, divided**
- ½ **cup pitted kalamata olives**
- ½ **cup crumbled feta cheese**
- 2 **teaspoons minced fresh thyme**

This is a wonderful side salad that's excellent with grilled fish, chicken, and just about anything else. The feta adds a wonderful saltiness to the mellow and slightly bitter zucchini. *Serves 4*

Prepare the grill to medium. In a large bowl, toss the zucchini with enough of the oil to coat the slices evenly. Grill the zucchini until lightly charred and cooked but still firm, 2 to 3 minutes per side. Transfer the grilled zucchini to a platter and top with the olives, cheese, thyme, and remaining oil. Serve immediately.

Raw Asparagus Salad with Toasted Walnuts & Mizithra

by Shauna James Ahern and Daniel Ahern, glutenfreegirl.com

One evening, Danny brought home a small wedge of Mizithra cheese. "Have you ever eaten this?" he asked me, extending a small slice of the salty, pungent cheese. "Of course!" I shouted. "At the Spaghetti Factory!" When I was a kid, we went to the Spaghetti Factory throughout the summer, after a long day at the beach. My father always ordered spaghetti with Mizithra and browned butter. When Danny and I started playing, we found that Mizithra, raw asparagus, toasted walnuts, and fresh tarragon leaves make an even better combination. If you can't find Mizithra, you can use Parmesan cheese in this recipe. *Serves 4*

Place the lemon juice, lemon zest, and kosher salt and pepper to taste in a small bowl and stir. Slowly add the oil, stirring to combine. Set the dressing aside.

Place the asparagus and tarragon in a large bowl. Add the dressing to taste and toss. Top with the toasted walnuts and cheese and serve.

¼ cup fresh lemon juice

1 tablespoon lemon zest
  Kosher salt and freshly ground black pepper

½ cup extra-virgin olive oil

1 bunch asparagus, trimmed and cut into ½-inch pieces

2 tablespoons fresh tarragon leaves

1 cup shelled walnuts, toasted (see Make It Easy)

¼ cup Mizithra cheese, shaved into small curls

MAKE IT EASY

To toast the walnuts, put the shelled walnuts in a large ovenproof sauté pan and slide it into a 350°F oven. After 10 minutes, toss the walnuts around a bit. Roast until the roasting smell fills the room, 5 to 10 more minutes.

Todd's Potato Pancakes
by Todd Porter and Diane Cu, **whiteonricecouple.com**

These potato pancakes are based on a recipe found in a favorite old cookbook that belonged to Todd's grandma. She gave the recipe a four-star rating, her highest mark.

The potato pancakes develop a beautiful, crispy outside and a soft, savory interior, and they make a great side for most main dishes. Be sure to make a few extra to munch on before serving them. *Serves 4*

Line a colander with a clean dish towel and grate the potatoes onto the towel. Fold over the towel and press down to squeeze out and drain the excess liquid. Transfer the potatoes to a large bowl. Add the onion, garlic, flour, sea salt, pepper to taste, and eggs, in that order, stirring to combine.

Heat the oil in a large sauté pan over medium-high heat. Working in batches, drop 4 portions of the potato batter into the pan; use a spatula to flatten each portion into a disk just under ½ inch thick. Fry until golden-brown, 2 to 3 minutes per side. Transfer the pancakes to an ovenproof dish and pat dry. Stir the remaining potato batter and repeat, adding more oil to the pan as needed.

Serve the potato pancakes warm, garnished with chives, if desired. They can be kept covered in a 300°F oven until ready to serve.

4 medium potatoes, peeled
½ large sweet onion, coarsely grated
3 garlic cloves, minced
⅓ cup all-purpose flour
¾ teaspoon sea salt
Freshly ground black pepper
2 large eggs, beaten
¼ cup peanut or canola oil, plus additional if needed
Chopped chives, for garnish

MAKE IT EASY
Try using an ice-cream scoop to portion out your batter—you'll end up with even portions and more uniform potato pancakes.

Side Dishes

Basil Corn *by Christy Jordan,* southernplate.com

1¾ pounds frozen corn kernels

8 tablespoons (1 stick) unsalted butter

1 tablespoon dried basil

1 tablespoon cornstarch

1 teaspoon sugar

½ teaspoon salt

I'm always looking for ways to season frozen vegetables and give them more of a garden-fresh flavor. My husband and I love corn and this is one of our favorite ways to serve it when we don't have fresh corn. It's very economical, too! *Serves 4*

Place the corn in a large pot and cover with water. Bring to a boil, remove from the heat, and drain. Transfer to a medium bowl and set aside.

Place the butter, basil, cornstarch, sugar, and salt in a medium saucepan over medium heat. Cook, stirring constantly, until the butter is completely melted and the mixture is well blended and bubbling. Add the butter mixture to the corn and stir to coat well. Serve immediately.

Quinoa Mexicana Salad *by Catherine McCord,* weelicious.com

In the summertime, I love to make this super-easy salad because it has loads of protein from the quinoa, tons of vitamins from all the veggies, and a gorgeous variety of colors that will catch everyone's eye. Try this as a side with chicken or beef. *Serves 4*

Place the quinoa and water in a medium saucepan and bring to a boil. Reduce the heat to low, cover, and simmer until the water is absorbed and the quinoa is tender, about 15 minutes. Transfer the quinoa to a medium bowl and let it cool for 5 minutes. Add the avocado, corn, tomatoes, cilantro, lime juice, and oil. Season to taste with salt, stir to combine, and serve.

½ cup quinoa, washed and drained
1 cup water
1 avocado, peeled, pitted, and chopped
½ cup fresh or frozen corn kernels, cooked
½ cup cherry tomatoes
2 tablespoons chopped fresh cilantro leaves
1 tablespoon fresh lime juice
1 tablespoon olive oil
¼ teaspoon ground cumin
Salt

MAKE IT EASY
Make extra quinoa for a next-day dinner, to serve with chicken or vegetables. Use scissors to cut the cilantro instead of chopping it with a knife.

Crispy Kale *by Jaden Hair,* steamykitchen.com

⅓ pound kale leaves, rinsed, dried, torn, center ribs and stems removed

1½ tablespoons olive oil

¼ teaspoon sea salt

This recipe works as a side dish or a snack, and it will get your kids to eat healthy, leafy kale!

The secret to a crispy, chiplike texture is drying the leaves thoroughly; moisture causes the kale to steam instead of bake. Dry the leaves by using a salad spinner and then blotting the leaves with paper towels. Also, don't salt the kale until after you've removed it from the oven.

Serves 4

Preheat the oven to 350°F. Line a baking sheet with parchment paper. Place the kale leaves on the parchment paper in a single layer. Drizzle the kale with the oil and, using your hands, toss gently to coat.

Bake until the kale leaves are crisp and the edges are golden, 10 to 12 minutes, checking frequently so the leaves do not brown and become bitter. Remove from the oven, season with the sea salt, and serve immediately.

MAKE IT EASY

Not sure if the kale is done? At the 10-minute mark, use a spatula or tongs to check: If the leaves are paper-thin and crackle, the kale is done. If the leaves are still a bit soft, let them cook for another couple of minutes.

Jaden Hair, steamykitchen.com

Jaden Hair is a television chef and food writer specializing in recipes that are fast, fresh, and simple enough for tonight's dinner. She is a weekly food columnist for Discovery's *TLC* and the *Tampa Tribune* newspaper. Jaden is a television chef on *The Daytime Show*, which is syndicated to over a hundred markets in the United States. She is the author of *The Steamy Kitchen Cookbook* and maintains the award-winning blog Steamy Kitchen (steamykitchen.com). She lives in Florida with her husband, Scott, and their sons, Andrew and Nathan.

More About Jaden

What do you always have in your shopping cart?
A knob of ginger and some kind of fruit. With my generous liquor cabinet and fresh mint growing in my backyard, I've always got a Mojito ready to go!

What's your go-to weeknight dinner?
I like to keep it simple and light—some nights it's just a loaf of crusty bread, a couple wedges of good stinky cheese, and shaved prosciutto.

What's your favorite kitchen tool?
Rubber-tipped tongs! I can flip, flop, nudge, turn, toss, lift.

Is there anything you just can't eat?
I've never turned down anything before. But then I've never traveled with Andrew Zimmern.

Grilled Sweet Potato Wedges with Cilantro Yogurt *by Matt Armendariz,* **mattbites.com**

1   **cup plain yogurt**
2   **tablespoons chopped fresh
    cilantro leaves**
1   **tablespoon fresh lime juice**
¼   **teaspoon salt, plus additional
    for seasoning**
2   **pounds medium red-skinned
    sweet potatoes (yams), each
    cut lengthwise into 6 wedges**
2   **tablespoons olive oil**
¼   **teaspoon cayenne pepper or
    ⅛ teaspoon curry powder
    Freshly ground black pepper**

This is a favorite at my house, and it is easy and goes with everything! The cool tang of the yogurt complements the sweetness of the potato. You can make the yogurt up to one day ahead, but plan to polish it off quickly. *Serves 4*

Place the yogurt, cilantro, lime juice, and salt in a medium bowl and stir to combine. Set the cilantro yogurt aside.

Prepare the grill to medium. Place the sweet potato wedges in a large pot of cold salted water and bring to a boil. Reduce the heat to medium-low and cook until the potatoes are almost tender, about 5 minutes.

Drain the potatoes and transfer to a large bowl; add the oil, cayenne pepper or curry powder, and salt and black pepper to taste. Toss gently to coat the potato wedges.

Grill the potato wedges over indirect heat, turning once, until tender and lightly charred, about 15 minutes. Serve warm with the cilantro yogurt.

index

Note: Page references in *italics* indicate photographs.